DATE DUE

NO 5 '96			
NO 26 96			
JY 30 '97			
MY 18 '99			
00			

DEMCO 38-296

Broken
Portraits

Broken Portraits

▶

Personal Encounters
with
Chinese Students

▶

Michael David Kwan

CHINA BOOKS & PERIODICALS • SAN FRANCISCO

Cover design by Laurie Anderson
Text design by Robbin Henderson

Library of Congress Catalog Card Number: 90-82644

ISBN 0-8351-2429-0 (casebound)
ISBN 0-8351-2381-2 (paperback)

Printed in the United States of America by CHINA
BOOKS
& Periodicals, Inc.

Dedicated to

RUSS, MARK, NICK, WENDY, & NANCY—
without whose love, understanding, and support this book
would not have been written;

and to
MY STUDENTS & FRIENDS —
whose story this is, but whose true identities have been
obscured for safety's sake;

and, finally, to
ABSENT FRIENDS.

Contents

Prologue

In the early hours of June 4, 1989, the 27th Army of the People's Republic of China unleashed its guns and tanks on unarmed students and citizens in the streets of Beijing as it pressed on to Tiananmen Square in the heart of the city. It was the first time since the establishment of the People's Republic in 1949 that the army was used on its own people in a massacre of unparalleled brutality. I was a scant twenty kilometers away, safe in a campus apartment for Foreign Experts when the killing took place. The aftershock of that night's bloody business is still felt.

Why did it happen?

Was it the panic of a venal old man who saw power and privilege he grasped so tenaciously slipping from his talons as mortality stared him in the face?

Was it impatient youth drunk with desire for change that pitched them on a collision course with the state?

Was it the convulsion of a sleeping giant waking to a world it never made?

It was all of those things.

For the student movement did not happen by chance. It grew out of events at times so remote as to seem unrelated. But the warning lights were flashing since the beginning of 1987 for anyone who cared to look.

Through its 5,000 years of continuous history China has been dominated by men who camouflaged their lust for power with ideals whose sound they liked better than their actuality. In China's odyssey through the ages, only the names of dynasties changed. Whether empire, republic, or socialist state, feudalism and its attendant corruption remained. Qin Shihuang* and Mao Zedong were driven by the same notions of personal and unlimited power. They could not succeed without the tacit approval of the masses. Perhaps there is a defect in the collective psyche of the Chinese people that allows them to be dragged ruthlessly through history without a whimper. Or perhaps the civilization is moribund and is no longer capable of growth.

One intellectual put it this way: "Chinese culture no longer exists. People are lazy and incapable of thought. We copy everything foreign and no longer produce anything that is ours whether in science, art, literature, or music."

An eminent novelist believes that China's greatest tragedy was not being conquered and colonized in the late nineteenth century. Said he, "We would have been carved into small manageable segments and we would have prospered under foreign rule." The same man concluded that China was due for another bloodbath. Only when its unwieldy population is whittled down to size can China begin to grow. This kind of cynicism would have earned the man a bullet in the head even before the tragedy on Tiananmen Square.

I was born in Beijing. My family left to make new lives in the West when Mao Zedong's armies swept away their affluent but gracious lifestyle. I was twelve years old. Yet my soul was rooted in China.

More than four decades later I returned to the city of my birth to teach. It was the spring of 1987. The grey city walls I remembered had given way to four wide sweeping Ring Roads. The tortuous lanes that were impassable quagmires when it rained were paved. Few of the courtyard houses that were a box within a box remain. Now people live in huge anonymous apartment blocks that are boxes stacked on boxes. My father's house had become part of Tiananmen Square.

* The emperor (259–210 B.C.) who unified China's separate states through war and annexation.

Life in Beijing is different from my childhood memories. There have been undeniable improvements for the masses. Everyone has a home, a job, food on the table, medical care, and children go to school.

But the standard of living is low compared to the West. The government's one child policy is bogged down by loopholes and inequalities between urban and rural communities. The population continues to burgeon. Often three or four generations live cheek by jowl, crammed into one or two rooms. Although such a "model family" is given a plaque which is proudly displayed on its front door, it is small comfort.

There were other problems. Agriculture suffered as farmers streamed into the cities lured by high-paying jobs on building sites. By the middle of 1988 Beijing was bursting at the seams. There were shortages. Pork, a mainstay of the Chinese diet, was once more on the ration list. Farmers refused to breed hogs because the escalating cost of feed and rigid price controls made it unprofitable. Sugar vanished from state-run grocery shelves. Ration coupons are needed to buy flour, rice, salt, oil, and even matches. However, everything is available on the free market at several times the proper price. But incomes have not caught up with these increases. Merchants refuse RMB (*renminbi*), the official currency of the realm, and insist on FEC (Foreign Exchange Certificates), which only foreign tourists are supposed to have. The result is a thriving black market in currency exchange.

There were rumblings of discontent.

Foreign Experts such as myself are paid in RMB and are issued a white card which entitles us to spend it. However, the ministry that issued the cards also instructed establishments we frequent not to honor them, or add 50 percent to the bill. In one stroke the state demolished its own myth that one FEC equals one RMB. It became almost impossible to walk along Changan Street between the diplomatic quarter and Jianguomen subway station without being accosted a dozen times by moneychangers, offering two-to-one for FEC. As winter set in, the moneychangers became bolder and more desperate. Some carried unsheathed knives as inducement when other persuasion failed.

Why this frenzy for FEC?

In the decade that China has been open to the West the people have been exposed to vacuum cleaners, color television, VCRs, refrigerators, and cars. Few can afford these luxuries but everybody wants them. All these things have to be paid for in FEC.

Most of all, FEC buys passports and visas to go abroad.

The last quarter of 1988 saw a dramatic change in attitudes of the general public. Inflation had reached two digits. People realized that things they desired were slipping further and further beyond their reach. Although supplements for food, transportation and other necessities are given, it is not universal. Intellectuals and teachers are not entitled.

Said one housewife to another on a crowded bus, "My food supplement buys me three bottles of yogurt a month!" Another waited twenty years for a five-yuan (just over one Canadian dollar) raise.

Bureaucratic corruption became a way of life. Nearly every day there are stories of official wrongdoing involving bribery, embezzlement, extortion and wasted resources. The *China Daily*, which delights in statistics, gleefully reports the thousands of cases that the state prosecutor's office has dealt with. Punishment is swift in China, and seldom fits the crime. Still it was a drop in the ocean. The real culprits were in government. Zhao Ziyang's two sons were reputed to be the worst racketeers in the country, but went scot-free. As the halfhearted clampdown made it inconvenient to take bribes that came gift-wrapped, the Chinese devised a new way to beat the system. Banqueting at public expense became all the rage. Lavish banquets were held at the drop of a hat. The nation went on an eating binge. Mao Tai, the fiery Chinese liquor, was selling at 186 yuan a bottle, equivalent to a professor's monthly salary. Yet it was consumed with gusto. Where did the money come from?

The economy was slipping into chaos. While Zhao Ziyang, the reformist secretary general of the Communist party trumpeted the virtues of continued opening to the West, and deepening reforms, the hard-liner Premier Li Peng advocated slowing down the economy. The contradictions became sharper all the time. One of the first signs of trouble was the shutting down of what were termed nonessential capital buildings. Huge projects were abandoned and left to rot. This included many grandiose joint venture hotels which were in various stages of construction. But it also included badly needed housing for a rapidly growing population.

Being a foreigner was no longer a guarantee of safety. Crime became more frequent and violent. Most foreigners were blissfully unaware of it, sheltered as they are from the realities by their cocoon existence on campuses and in hotels. I too led a sheltered life of sorts. But being completely bilingual I listened to conversations, read newspapers, magazines and the bits of clandestine protest that appeared on walls and lampposts around the city. A kind of desperation crept into the life of Beijing. It reminded me of some Monty Python film where a big foot was poised in the sky, waiting to squash the unwary. That big foot in the sky was already hovering over our heads at the beginning of the term in September '88.

Something was brewing out there.

My institute had an enrollment of two thousand and a faculty of one thousand, yet some courses had to be abandoned because there was no one to teach them. Faculty members who found ways of going abroad, left. Others worked as desk clerks and guides at tourist hotels, earning FEC, while still collecting their regular salaries. Everybody who can, moonlights. One professor I knew has not taught for over two years. Many of those who do appear before their classes have taught the same material so long, they do it in their sleep. Their disinterest is infectious. The students who enter the institute with high hopes are quickly disillusioned when courses are either not available or given so lackadaisically as to be meaningless. But worst is when they finally realize they have no control over their lives. D—, a lanky young man is always tinkering with things. He has a knack for fixing mechanical devices but neither an ear for nor interest in languages. He should be in a technical school. Instead, the state has sent him to the institute to study English and tourism. When he graduates, he will be a tour guide if he is lucky. If not, he will go home to a small town in central China and be a schoolteacher. D— is in the wrong field, but there is no recourse. Although students are asked their preferences when they write their college entrance exams, few are assigned according to their personal interests. There is no possibility for change once they are assigned. At home, the student is often pressured into a career that parents have chosen out of self-interest. Under the veneer of socialism, China is still a feudal society.

The lack of facilities for the care of the aged has pushed them into the laps of the next generation. Parents look upon children as insurance against the day when they can no longer earn their keep. Thus they bind their children to themselves by refusing to let them grow up. For many young people, going to college was the first time they were away from parents. The experience was traumatic at first, because they had never fended for themselves before. But once they got used to it, a whole new world opened up to them. In the colleges, along with foreign technology the young have acquired rock and roll, tight jeans, brightly colored T-shirts, punk hair styles, nightclubs, Rambo, Sydney Sheldon novels, and break-dancing. Some have been induced to think for themselves. Tantalized by half-understood Western philosophies, youth seethed with discontent. D— is typical of so many young men and women of China.

Jobs are assigned upon graduation. For example, a student enters the institute to study economics with a view of a career in foreign trade. At the end of four years he or she is in for a rude awakening. The student who hopes to make it on ability alone seldom gets anywhere. It is not what you know but who you know, or who Ma and Pa know that matters. The best jobs go to students from cadre families. Then to party members who have demonstrated their worthiness. D— bowed to the wishes of parents, and found himself trapped for life. His one possible escape is to join the Party. If he minds his P's and Q's, and butters up the right people, he might get a better job assignment when he graduates. If he bides his time and works hard he might get a chance to go abroad. It is the dream of escape that keeps D— going. The tragedy is that D— does not want to leave China. He firmly believes in her potential. But he feels stifled by society, and can find neither understanding nor comfort from grasping parents. The bitter conflict between the generations has become increasingly pronounced.

For the vast majority of students the will to excel and the desire to acquire knowledge is quickly destroyed. Cynicism sets in. Life becomes a grey nothingness. Many cut classes altogether to work the black market and accumulate money, for Money is the only god worth worshiping. Others sink into a morass of self-pity and despair. The socialism they have been nurtured on since early childhood has become suspect; a diseased thing that can no longer be relied upon to produce the good life. But there is nothing to take its place. Yet when minds eroded by boredom and monotony suddenly catch fire it is exciting, and exceedingly rewarding. The criminal waste of young potential was one of the causes that sparked the student movement.

The presence of Foreign Experts adds to the prestige of an institution. Ours had a fairly large and international group from Britain, France, Belgium, Spain, Germany, the USSR, Egypt, Japan, the United States, and Canada.

There is a world of difference between the life of a Foreign Expert and that of a native professor or student. It does not take much perception to realize that Foreign Experts are really window dressing for the school. The majority of Foreign Experts are more interested in traveling and treat it as a paid holiday. The few who take their work seriously are frustrated by the lack of equipment and cooperation. Foreign Experts are seldom included in any campus functions. They are uninformed about curricula or extra-curricular activities. They stand before their classes day after day, but few get to know their students. An invisible wall separates them, part of which is a language barrier. The first university I taught at housed me in a hotel far from campus. Distance alone was an effective deterrent to any contact outside the classroom. At the institute it was different. Living on campus made it possible to associate with students. Nevertheless barriers still existed which I was loath to break down at the outset. For one thing, I did not know how friendship with a foreigner might affect the students' futures. Thus it was left to their discretion. However, I was fortunate that a group eventually grew around me. We talked, we argued, we laughed and sang, ate and drank together. I refused to discuss two topics: politics and religion. And I was careful not to paint the Western world in hues too rosy in or out of the classroom.

Foreign Experts are housed in a four-story building with all the amenities of home. Separated from us by a playing field is the dormitory for boys, where ghetto-blasters blare a mixture of hard rock and John Denver schmaltz from dawn to late at night. Seven students live in one tiny eight-by-ten-foot room with just enough space for four bunk beds, and a small desk and chair. Two rows of rooms face each other across a dark and dingy hall lit by tiny windows at each end. Most of the light bulbs have burnt out long ago and not been replaced. The air is unbreathable and the reek from toilets at either end of the hall permeates the building. On each floor there is a "water room" with a row of cement troughs and faucets. This is for washing and laundry. There are no showers. The bathhouse is situated on the opposite end of campus and open between certain hours.

The girls living on the opposite side of the field in a similar building are in equally squalid conditions. One could almost say their lot is worse. The boys have a building that is only six months old. The girls' dorm dates from the '50s.

Meals are taken in a huge, drafty, echoing cement barn. Aside from the playing field, there are no recreational facilities. On Wednesday nights there is a movie. Usually a double-bill of kung-fu from Hong Kong and a soppy romance from Taiwan. On Saturday night there is a dance.

I think of my students as boys and girls. But they are

actually young men and women, though less mature than their Western counterparts. Most have never been away from parents, never coped with the day-to-day realities of life, never associated with the opposite sex. Most of them have never made an independent decision. Suddenly there is no one to tell them what to do. That is not to say there are no rules. There are rules in plenty, but their enforcement is left to whim. For instance, there is a rule against dating. But it happens all the time, and a few illicit pregnancies too. There is a rule against gambling, but mahjong is played day and night. Once in a while the administration takes a stand and a few offenders are rounded up and expelled. But it's business as usual the day after.

Not long ago D— said to me, in a moment of black despair, "I am almost twenty-five years old. But I have never had a date, never been in love, never had sex, never been really happy or really sad. My life is nothing." The outburst startled me. D— had always been shy, partly because his English was not as good as it should have been. But even in Chinese he said very little, though one had the impression that a lot went on behind those hooded eyes. What came afterwards made me really take notice. "Soon I may be dead," he said with a kind of finality that I was to hear again and again. "I am not afraid; just sorry because I've never really lived."

The next day D— joined the hunger strike.

Part One

▶

Storm Warning

1

▶

13 September 1988   From my window I can watch white sailboats gliding across the mirror-flat sea. This old house creaks and groans. I wander through the rooms touching this and that, as if feeling the texture of things would bring them closer to me. But it doesn't. The little cat trots over and rubs herself against my leg. I stroke her and she purrs, looking up at me with wide accusing eyes. "You're leaving me again," they say.

"You don't have to go again," a good friend said on the phone a moment ago. "You've already been there and done that. There's nothing to prove."

There isn't, of course. Then what is driving me back to China? Roots, I suppose. I was born in China, and China is in my blood. Going back to roots is 90 percent emotion and 10 percent reason. Suddenly there are two of me.

Reason says, "This is madness! It is downright irresponsible. When you come back your career will be up the flue. And at your age it will be too late to start over again."

Emotion says, "If you don't go you will end up a bitter, lonely old man who never really lived. Live your life."

So, here I am, smoking my last pipe, my things in a neat pile by the door. Books, pictures, antiques, records, tapes, furniture, this house—none of it seems to have any connection with me any more. My red Toyota is gone from the driveway. The only new car I ever owned, or ever will, was sold last week. In the same week, the swallow's nest that has occupied the western corner of the eaves under the porch fell during a storm. Woodstock and his mate sat on the telephone line for a long time chirping disconsolately at each other. Finally they flew away. There is a belief in the East that swallows only nest where there is a home. Perhaps some intelligence beyond our ken told the swallows that soon this place will only be a house. My sons have all found their niches. One has already gone; the other two will leave in due course.

It is time to go.

I turned the key in the front door one more time. I did not look back when the taxi pulled away from the curb. This place is too deeply ingrained to need a backward glance.

A few years ago a psychic, an old Scottish woman, told me I would go to China many times; that it would change my life.

This is the second time; and it has changed my life.

16 September 1988

MY DEAR RUSS & WENDY,

The flight to Beijing was long and tedious. One can't expect much on the world's worst airline. The boxed meals were as sour as the stewardesses. I can see I have my work cut out for me teaching tourism. I sat next to "Madge"* and husband. They were part of a strange group from Victoria on a seven-day "pilgrimage" to all the places where St. Norman Bethune walked. Just what they were is hard to say. But they had the scrubbed, boiled, and starched look, and a crusading air about them that makes me uncomfortable. "Madge," fortyish, thin-lipped and humorless walked straight out of a Norman Rockwell picture. "Mr. Madge," who wore enough gold chains and earrings for the both of them, hid behind a bushy beard looking soulful. I deliberately asked for an aisle seat. How was I to know that I would end up beside

---

* "Madge" is a term for tourists who are loud, opinionated, ignorant, and often obnoxious in a self-righteous way. "Madge" was invented by my son, Russel.

two weak bladders and in the direct path of the stampede to the loo? During the first hour out I thought I would be trampled to death, as first one, then the other, trotted up the aisle.

Finally they settled down. Madge had not done her homework. Now she had just twelve hours to digest the life of Bethune. She read with a fierce concentration, her eyes following the tip of her finger which slowly moved across the page. Mr. Madge watched the silly movie, grunting testily at Madge's asides. Madge skipped to the last part of the book and whined at spouse, whose eyes remained resolutely glued to the screen.

I leaned into my seat and flipped through the in-flight magazine. Two photographs in an article on Toronto caught my eye. One was of a nondescript old house, whose caption read: "Toronto city." Beside it was a photograph of skyscrapers, overpasses, and traffic jams, captioned, "Birthplace of Dr. Norman Bethune." For some silly reason, the switched captions amused me. I showed it to Madge, who had been gulping and sighing over the life and times of NB the last half hour. She was not amused. *Mea culpa . . . mea culpa . . . mea MAXIMA culpa . . .* Anything associated with NB was sacrosanct.

"He's a saint!" she sighed to no one in particular, dabbing at wet eyes.

"He's a drunk." I retorted. I'm afraid I really endeared myself to poor Madge who stared at me in disbelief.

"He's a great doctor!" she pronounced, in a voice that rumbled like an organ in an empty church.

"He's a fraud!" I was in a devilish mood. Saint Norman Bethune wobbled on his pedestal. Madge was getting hot under the collar.

"He went to China!" she said, as if that proved anything.

"He had nowhere else to go!" I said. I thought Madge would explode. She screwed her eyes into tiny slits, and her mouth twisted itself into impossible shapes.

"Why are you going to China?" she hissed.

"I have nowhere else to go either," I said. Madge charged off to the loo in a huff. Mr. Madge winked at me. One should show more respect, I suppose, but these intense types get to me.

Wonder of wonders, CACA* was thirty minutes early getting in! It was almost midnight and everybody was anxious to get out of immigration and customs. There was the usual melee and not a pushcart to be had. There I was with a pack on my back, laptop computer slung over one shoulder, printer under one arm, and dragging a heavy duffel bag with the other. A bored young customs officer took one look at this apparition, curled his lip, and muttered, "Get out of my life."

Outside, a swarm of taxi-drivers descended on me. Just six months ago they would have sat in their cabs picking their noses. Here they were hustling! "Come with me . . . come with me . . . " one fellow tugged at my sleeve. I clutched my pockets instinctively, nearly dropping the printer. You can't be too careful these days. . . "Anywhere you want—FEC," he smiled, drowning me in garlic breath. Foreign Exchange Certificates makes their eyes gleam. They swarmed all over me like locusts. I fended them off as best I could, all the while trying to pick out the person who was to meet me from the passing crowd. People went by flashing pieces of paper with names scrawled on them. I staggered to a public address booth and asked if they would page the person.

The woman in the booth was not overjoyed. They never are when they are asked to do their job. "What name?" she asked without enthusiasm. She was absorbed in a magazine. I told her and I waited. "What do you want?" she asked, tearing herself away from what she was reading.

"Would you please page that person?" She waved ten red lacquered fingernails in the air. "Can't. My nails are wet." We glared at each other in silence. Since I showed no inclination either to go away or stop staring at her, she eventu-

---

* A huge billboard near the Beijing Zoo reads, "Fly CACA—Customey and Savety First." I pointed out this curious advertisement to an official in tourism who shrugged and said, "Who cares!" However, the foreign community has taken this adventure to heart. "Fly CACA" describes their opinion of the airline very accurately.

ally complied. By then "Madge" and company had piled into a bus and roared off into the night. The crowd thinned. Even the taxi drivers evaporated. I was beginning to be concerned. Suddenly, a young man clattered past, galloping after someone getting into a cab, waving a piece of paper with my name on it. Was I glad to see him! Wang, who has been assigned as my assistant, was so used to CACA being late, was thirty minutes late himself. He apologized all the way to campus.

17 September 1988

DEAR MARK & NICK,

Campus is way out in the sticks, between the Great Wall Hotel and the airport, almost two hours by public bus to the center of town and Tiananmen Square. But it is pleasant to be part of the real world, away from the hothouse atmosphere of the Friendship Hotel. The institute is sandwiched between two highways that link Beijing to the seaport of Tianjin. The one to the north, which is being widened into four lanes, looks like a bomb site. The Chinese do not repair roads in sections. They dig up the whole length. The north road is mile upon mile of open trench in which sewage collects in horrid black pools on which tiny green things float. The fumes make you gag. Traffic is mostly diverted to the south road whose two narrow lanes are choked with a never-ending stream of buses, jitneys, bicycles, trucks, and mule carts. The noise, the dust, the heat, and the stench are already familiar. It seems I have never been away at all.

I am comfortably settled into my new digs. I have a huge ground floor apartment that faces south. Outside is a small yard which could be quite attractive. But the Chinese have no notion of mowing the grass, which is waist high, and full of pink and purple wild flowers. Crickets thrive in the millions out there; sopranos, tenors, altos, and basses chirping their little hearts out. It's a wonder some enterprising soul hasn't swooped down on them net in hand. Fighting crickets are worth the price of a racehorse in China. Beyond the yard is a building site. Where can one look in Beijing without encountering a building going up?

My front door opens onto a foyer/dining area. To the left is a living room/study, lined on one side by a wall unit (Ikea with Chinese characteristics) with bookshelves and cupboards from floor to ceiling. On the other side of the room is a sectional sofa and arm chair in red velvet and a long coffee table. Under the windows are a long desk and typing table. Next to the living room is the bedroom which is the same size, with two single beds, lots of closet space, and a second desk. The Manet print and the poster of western Australia which you gave me adorn the livingroom walls. The bullfight poster Mark brought home from Mexico is in the dining area. Ludwig (Beethoven) glowers from the bedroom wall. My books are on the shelves, and there are photographs here and there.

There is an old fashioned tub with clawed feet in the bathroom. The water pipes shake, rattle and roll but everything works. However, I shall have to take a wire brush to the floor one of these days when I am properly motivated.

My large kitchen is fitted with a fridge, and a gas stove and oven. Actually, it's quite a nifty little stove: two burners and an oven just wide enough for a chicken. However, it is not functional, as the gas has not been connected.

Every morning people come to look at the stove. This morning eight men jammed into the kitchen, all yelling at the same time. Half an hour later they trooped out muttering and frowning. I noticed a smell of gas and pointed it out. "Everything's fine," said Chang, a little man with a big voice and an outsized grin who is the jack-of-all-trades around the building. I suppose the gas will get properly connected as long as they're yelling at each other. It's the silences that are worrying.

This is luxury. Most Chinese families live in a quarter of the space and cook on charcoal braziers.

16 September 1988   Today I bought a ghetto blaster—a Philips assembled in China—and the place begins to feel like home.

17 September 1988   I have—not one—but two assistants!
W— who came to fetch me at the airport, and S—. W— is an
earnest young man with a face full of pockmarks and bright
beady eyes behind thick lenses. W— teaches English and
speaks very well. He has already been abroad twice in his
short life. Papa used to be an attaché at an embassy "somewhere in Europe." Probably one of the Eastern bloc coun-
tries. W— loves to travel, and is absolutely fascinated by my
poster of Manet's Venice. "Is it really like that?" he asked.

Venice is one of my favorite places. Listening to myself
waxing lyrical I suddenly realized how unreal the rest of the
world has become. Even Venice seems more a mirage than
a real city. Only China is real. But the reverse operates for
W—.

W— and I spent the whole afternoon tramping from one
end of the city to the other tracking down a box of teaching
materials I shipped ahead. It was a maze of red tape and
rubber stamps that I could not have navigated without him.
W— knows when to smile, frown, cajole, and hand out
cigarettes. Now the books were scattered all over the floor,
forgotten, while we talked about Venice.

"I could have gone there," W— said wistfully.

I waited for something more. But that was it. Conversation with Chinese people tends to suffer sudden deaths. A
curtain is drawn abruptly, without reason. W— finished his
tea and left.

The next day, S— appeared on the doorstep and introduced himself as my "other assistant." W— had gone off to
work as a tour guide. "But I thought he teaches English?" I
asked, surprised. S— shrugged. Everybody is doing some
other job, he said, with a note of envy in his voice. S— is a
Manchu with the typical high forehead, flat features, and
narrow eyes, enlarged by glasses. S— is an owlish fellow,
whose halting, heavily accented English is hard to follow.
After a while we switch to Chinese. He was noticeably
relieved and the conversation became more animated. S—
reminds me of an overgrown St. Bernard puppy who is
anxious to please.

He phones every morning to see if there is anything I need done. Yesterday, I casually mentioned that I wanted to see the dean to discuss the course I am giving. The next thing I knew, the dean was on my doorstep. The protocol was all wrong. I must watch what I say to this eager beaver! It was embarrassing.

18 September 1988   I went in search of the dean. We have already exchanged the usual pleasantries on arrival, but we had not talked about the specifics of my work here. Campus is really quite attractive. There are many large trees, and pleasantly secluded nooks and corners where students read aloud to themselves, committing everything to memory. Or creating memories of their own.

I vaguely remembered the location of the administration building, having visited the institute more than six months before. But my poor sense of direction played tricks on me and it was a while before I finally bumbled my way to the right building. As I was going up the stairs, a young man in a black suit and white shirt open at the neck was coming down. He smiled toothily, eyes scrunched up into little slits. "You must be the new foreign teacher!" he exclaimed, extending his hand. We shook hands. He tossed the lock of stiff black hair out of his eyes. "Welcome! But you are late! We've been waiting! When do we begin classes?" All the while he still held onto my hand. Chinese handshakes sometimes linger uncomfortably.

"How did you know who I am?" I asked.

"I'm your student," he said. "The best. I'm Willie." He seemed bright, friendly and unshy.

"I'm pleased to meet you," I said. I recovered my hand after another extended handshake.

"I will take you to the dean," said Willie. We started up the stairs. Willie seemed to know everybody going up or down. It was recess. "How about my English?" he asked. "Is it well?"

"Is it GOOD?" I corrected. I could have bitten my tongue.

"Is it good?" Willie repeated without batting an eyelash.

"Very good," I said.

Willie smiled and clapped me on the shoulder. "I am your best student, and you will give me very good marks." They are all obsessed with marks.

"If you work hard, Willie." He looked blankly at me. But we had arrived at our destination. The dean's handshake is bone crushing. He is a pleasant man with one of those lined and craggy faces that will be a photographer's dream in another ten years. He was an army drill sergeant, and does not know a word of English. Nor does he know anything about tourism.

This four-year tourism program is rather astounding. The first three are spent learning English and another language—French, Japanese, etc., etc. The last year is tourism. They've had a number of foreigners in the past but none was qualified. Worst of all, none of them could communicate with the dean. So I am really given the kid gloves treatment.

My course outline lay on his desk. Prof. C—, who joined us, did all the talking—in English. There was a stark difference between the two men. The dean with his deeply furrowed, weather-beaten face and his grey Mao suit, and C—, with his horn-rimmed glasses, his soft white hands, and his shiny Italian silk suit, inhabited different worlds. C— was full of compliments on the course outline. The dean nodded and smiled sagely but even before C— said quite casually, "The dean doesn't know English," I more or less guessed that was the case. C— made a few references to the other's army career and the fact that he was not an academic as though he were talking about someone who was not in the room. I decided I did not like this C—. Finally he rose, shook hands, and bustled off.

"Is he my co-teacher?" I asked after the door closed on C—. The dean shook his head and smiled. "You're on your own," he said.

I have a free hand developing the course. A quick tour of the departmental reading room showed me just how lacking the institute was in material. There wasn't even a decent atlas. Tariffs and guides were unheard of. But there were tomes such as *Marxist Economics in Tourism*. I came prepared to write the material I teach. It was impossible to do any-thing more than an outline, as I had no idea of the level of English comprehension I would confront. If they are all as competent as young Willie, I will be pleasantly surprised. But that is not likely. Before long we were joined by Profes-sor L—, the department's political head. L— has a row of huge buck-teeth. His bearing betrays his military origins. He chain-smokes but did not proffer cigarettes. The dean remarked, apropos of nothing, "I've quit." "How come?" I asked, recalling that he too was a chain-smoker when we first met last year. In fact, his finger tips are still stained with nicotine. "It's too expensive these days," he explained. L— puffed silently and did not comment. The talk went to the distribution to students of material I am writing. Eventu-ally, all this material will be gathered up and published in book form. It will be the first tourism text written for China. In the meantime, students will have to receive it chapter by chapter. Although the department has a xerox machine, they prefer not to use it, the rationale being that the less it's used the less it's likely to break down. I tried to point out that the machine would deteriorate from disuse, and it would be a greater waste. The dean looked thoughtful. L— smiled. Neither really understood.

L— pointed out the print shop charges seventy-one cents a page and wanted to know how many pages I anticipated turning out. I threw up my hands. "Let's say enough for forty-four weeks."

That seemed to satisfy him. I have the impression that L— holds the purse strings. I point out that once the work was done, the institute would have a textbook that could be sold. Of course revisions would have to be made from time to time. But that is still way down the road. After kicking the problem back and forth a while, the solution was that a limited number of copies—five or six perhaps—would be produced and kept in the students' reading room in the library to be shared by seventy students. It was the best bargain I could make.

I have my work cut out for me. I teach eight hours a week on Tuesday, Thursday, and Friday. The seniors whom I have for tourism three times a week are a class of seventy. In addition, I've had a group of juniors foisted on me too. This lot I see once a week for something called "English for Tourism." It is a conversation course, but with fifty students, it is unwieldy and ineffective.

As the dean remarked, it's a lot of work. But I feel good about it.

Willie emerged from the shadows of the corridor as I left the dean's office. "I will show you the campus," he said, taking my arm. I must get used to being guided about as though I was a doddering old man. Here it is merely good manners.

With Willie's help I am beginning to find my way around the campus. The Foreign Experts' Building where I live is a four-story affair with balconies fore and aft, situated in a cul-de-sac at the western end of campus. Catty-corner to us to the north is a gleaming white building that is not quite finished. I am told it might become the girls' dormitory. Behind our building, facing my apartment across the plot of rank growth that passes for a lawn, is another gleaming white building which is almost finished. There seems to be some difference of opinion as to what it will be. There is always an uncomfortable element of surprise where accommodation is concerned in China.

East of that is a noisy building where the foreign students live. Across from the foreign students' building is an ugly red brick affair which houses the boys. Across a pleasant but narrow strip of garden where shade trees form a green canopy over the pathways is an identical building that houses the girls.

Behind the boys' dormitory is large quadrangle bounded by the new building on the west, the sinister-looking three-story clinic and party offices on the east and classroom building 2. The school looks as though it was built at the turn of the century. But it actually went up in the late '50s! The exteriors are quite presentable. The grey bricks set off the red window frames and doors, and the curved eves of the roof give the place a definite Chinese touch. The architecture is primitive. Long narrow hallways with rooms on either side, lit by windows at both ends. The hallways are plunged in permanent twilight. The cement walls and floors are icy in the winters. The stench of the latrines permeates the building.

Classroom building 1 used to be the library until the new one opened last year. Now there are two or three large lecture rooms on the ground floor and the upper floors have been converted to dormitories for post graduate students.

Classroom building 3 is at the eastern extremity of campus, forming a triptych of three relatively new buildings with the library and the audio-visual center. A cluster of gleaming white in the surrounding drabness of grey and dull red brick. The trees are still in leaf but there are touches of yellow. When the winter winds begin, it will be stark.

There is another group of low buildings across the road from the clinic. The closest to classroom building 3 is the restaurant for the Chinese faculty. They say the food there isn't what it used to be since the chef has been moved to the Foreign Experts' Dining hall. Then there is the bathhouse, which is used by Chinese students and staff. The students' club, which no longer functions except for the Wednesday night movies, is next. The last is a squat two-story building that serves as students' dining hall on the ground level and a reading room which was closed when the new library opened. There is also a tuck shop where smokes and booze are sold along with notepads, candies, and socks.

There is a playing field with a cinder track that is separated from the highway to the south by a low brick wall. There are several basketball courts and volleyball courts, and tennis courts without nets. That's campus.

Willie and I sat in the bleachers facing the running track. There were a few joggers out. A woman was practicing *qigong* (an ancient Chinese form of exercise that combines elements of yoga, martial arts, and harnessing *qi*, an energy force in the body that is held by some even to have psycho-kinetic power). The woman moved in a slow, trance-like dance, eyes tight shut. Suddenly she let out a blood-curdling scream and flailed the air as if she were beating off an invisible attacker. Then as if struck she fell to the ground and thrashed about, kicking up a great cloud of dust. The joggers went by without changing their pace. The woman writhed on the ground emitting the most hideous shrieks. "Is she all right?" I asked my young companion.

"She is giving off . . ." Willie groped for the word in English, and finally resorted to the Chinese, *qi*, which means air, or breath, but in this case means a form of energy. I have heard of this but had never seen it done.

"Who is she? You know her?" I must have looked blank.

"She is in charge of the departmental reading room."

"You mean the quiet one, with the short hair—shy?"

". . . Not very good looking," Willie finished for me. "But kindhearted." The woman had stopped writhing and screaming. She got to her feet, covered with dirt. Her knee protruded from a tear in her sweat pants. But even under the grime, her face glowed with an almost beatific serenity. "She has a husband and a child, but no friends," said Willie. "She does not allow people in her home," he finished, rather sourly. I guess he had been refused entry. "She only eats one meal a day. The *qi* gives her all the energy she needs," Willie went on.

"A good way to save," I remarked flippantly. "You should try it."

"Oh, no." Willie's eyes go round when he is serious. "I like to eat."

20 September 1988

Dear Gregory,

It has been two eventful weeks. I am settled into my new apartment and my work schedule, although I am still finding my way around the sprawling campus. Both my two assistants vanished after the first week. There was really little they could do for me that I couldn't do myself. And somewhere on the campus I have an office. But the dean said it is noisy there and I would be better off working in my apartment. So I left it for a while. Just the same, I had the key and I was curious. One morning when I had no classes, I went to explore. The office is huge, one door down from the dean's. The four desks and chairs have been pushed into the far corner, leaving a large empty space at the top end of the room. Dusty streamers hung limply from the ceiling. Indeed, a fine layer of dust covered everything, including the one decent piece of furniture, a black leather sofa. There was a flask of hot water and cups on the coffee table, and a chess table. The dust-free condition of the latter pieces of furniture, and the fact that the water in the flask was piping hot, would indicate that somebody plays chess, drinks tea, and has parties in "my office." I'll continue to work in my apartment.

20 September 1988 Life has settled down to a dull roar. There was the usual welcoming banquet last week. S— came with the invitation, grinning and bobbing his head. "You will attend?" "Of course," I said. It would be unthinkable not to. Besides the food at these functions is usually excellent. "It will be in your dining hall." S— made a face. "They're saving money." Why not? There are approximately thirty Foreign Experts here. Quite an international group, predominantly Japanese, with the usual complement of Americans, two Brits, a very large and jolly woman from Victoria, a mannish Aussie woman who is really quite nice, a moody Belgian woman who wears black leather, a hearty German woman of the exhausting variety, a Spanish woman who looks like a gypsy and has been in China thirty years, and a dour Russian woman who speaks French. Everybody gets along with everybody else so far. The Japanese are a very clannish lot. They travel in a group. Perhaps there is a language problem, but in the week we have been here they have made no attempt to get to know the rest of us. A couple who look very nice live in the apartment above me. We pass each other in the hallway all the time. We smile and bow, and murmur, *"Ni hao* (good day)." But that is all. Every Saturday night they have a real Japanese bath, and the water floods through to my bathroom. Otherwise, they are nice quiet neighbors.

Dick and Maisy live one floor above them. He is from a middle-class suburb of Toronto. She is one of the Lanskys of Duluth. Just who and what they are is a mystery. He has the haunted look of a defrocked priest. Or one that has left the church. Catholic priests have an indefinable air that is instantly recognizable. She has a mass of reddish, somewhat wiry curly hair and speaks through her nose. She was probably spoiled silly as a child, and has a way of curling her lips when she speaks that gives her an unpleasant sneering look. He is a writer, but thus far has been waiting for that magic moment when inspiration will strike like a bolt of lightning. Sounds familiar. She taught at an "exclusive" boys' school. Dick and Maisy teach English and literature respectively. "We really don't have any expectations of these Chinese students," announced Dick. He is given to pompous statements when her ladyship is within earshot. But they do their darnedest to bring culture and a dash of high society to the building. They have been dubbed "Their Eminences."

Gladys is an Aussie with a high complexion and boundless energy. She is about my age, mid-fifties if she is a day. She would think nothing of sitting on the floor of a crowded Chinese train overnight to save a few pennies, but she too puts on hoity-toity airs. She's the Kangaroo Princess.

The three single American men are all peculiar. Donald who lives above "Their Eminences" is a loner from Oregon. He has the pale blue eyes of Paul Newman but that is where the resemblance ends. Donald is very intelligent, has a masters in literature, but has never taught until he came to China a year ago. He has been a biker, a soldier in Vietnam, and a hospital orderly. At age forty plus, he still refers to his parents as Mummy and Daddy. Apparently an only child of their old age, Donald was intimidated by Daddy, who was a military type, and smothered by Mummy. Daddy died when Donald was in his teens. That might have been liberating except Mummy was there. Last year while he was in China, Mummy suddenly died. Donald has not been able to cope with Mummy's demise. He stays pretty much to himself. He makes me nervous when he practices T'ai Chi with a sword. A strange demented look comes into his eyes. I fear he might either harm himself or another person one of these days.

Bill is from New York. Thinning red hair, a face full of freckles, and if it wasn't for the lisp and the limp wrist, might have been the Van Johnson type of American boy next door. The first time we met in the dining hall, he rolled his eyes at me and fluted, "Well, where did YOU come from?" Bill has the openness of a child. But he is a tiresome braggart who takes the title of Foreign Expert very seriously. He is an expert on every subject under the sun. He lived in France and is a master of French cuisine. He is the only person I've ever met who's made chocolate rolls on the Riviera. He was a clerk at a university with which the institute has an exchange program. So here he is, teaching English. But his real interest is young Chinese men.

Marc lives only five blocks from Bill in New York. One can't hope to find a more neurotic person, even in New York. Marc despises "Miss Bill" and delights in mimicking his lisp. He is a full-fledged teacher who taught in a ghetto school in Brooklyn, and there is a tough side to him that I do not like. He is brittle and given to spectacular rages, usually directed at people who cannot defend themselves, such as students. Otherwise, it is a caustic tongue that stings. Yet there are good points to the man too. For some peculiar reason he has singled me out as a friend. Yet it is the sort of friendship that I feel will not last. Marc is exclusive and monopolistic, and one cannot live that way in this closed society. Most people who come to China are running from something or running towards something. I wonder what it is that drove Marc here.

Greta's hair is cropped shorter than a boy's. She has one of those complexions that would put the manufacturers of make-up out of business. But the lady is tough. She wears black leather even to a banquet, and rides a motorcycle to class.

Birgit came to China to be with her husband, who works for a German trading company. A life of leisure in Beijing can jangle the nerves, so she ended up teaching German. She is a cheerful energetic woman whose refinements such as declaiming Goethe and singing Schubert, and producing astonishing dessert using a bare minimum of materials and equipment, have naturally gravitated her toward the inner circle of Their Eminences.

Veronica, the only other Canadian, is very large and jolly. The earth mother type who takes everything in her stride, she is an organizer. Birthdays and festivals never slip by. She even managed to worm Woody's birthday out of him and organized a surprise party for the occasion. Of course Woody had to be cajoled into coming. But he did. Veronica is also a real teacher.

Then there is little Mr. Ito. How could I forget Mr. Ito! We had been neighbors for a whole year at the Friendship Hotel, and I caught the worst case of bronchitis of my life rooming with him on a weekend trip. Mr. Ito had a dumpy little wife who always walked three paces behind him and never spoke unless she was spoken to. She must have gone home to Japan, for Ito-san is alone. Still some things never change. Mr. Ito always wears kimonos, even to his classes. Mr. Ito is the only Japanese teacher I can communicate with, after a fashion. He speaks Chinese. However, I have a feeling his Chinese is a lot better than he would like people to know.

Finally there is Edward, a very blond and pink young Brit who looks like a mere kid, and blushes furiously when he is spoken to. Edward—not Ed or Eddy or Teddy—is obviously older than he looks, and something of a linguist. He speaks French, and insists on speaking Chinese to me in a dreadful accent. I cringe when people practice on me instead of making conversation. Unfortunately Edward is one of those. And he got my back up from the start. But he really is a harmless sort. He is another one that looks as though he belongs in a seminary, and like Dick, doesn't drink. I am suspicious of people who don't drink. Especially here.

There is also quite a large foreign student population. Again the Japanese outnumber the rest. There are a few Americans—three to be exact—two Baptists and one

Mormon—a few (reputedly) promiscuous French, a very blonde and handsome German, and a handful of Russians who are chaperoned. The students live in a building next to ours. Their building has a pub but no dining hall. So we swap. For some strange reason the students are always hungry. At least they behave as though they hadn't eaten for the last five days, or perhaps they think they're locusts. Anyway, they swoop down on the dining hall as soon as it opens, and fifteen minutes later everything is *mayo*—all gone!

The motley crew gathered in the dining hall. The tables were laid with fresh white cloths and small vases of silk flowers. The same orange, yellow, and purple ones that used to grace the tables of the Friendship Hotel. I sat between the dean and the vice president. One plied me with food and the other with drink. The conversation was desultory as a great deal of attention was paid to the food which kept coming. It was very good. The old chef, who had been pointed out to me, used to work in a leading restaurant in Hangzhou and had been brought to Beijing after his retirement, "especially for our foreign friends." There were many speeches. Y— of the foreign affairs office kept bobbing up to translate. It's a wonder the poor woman had anything to eat! Each speech ended with a toast. It was not Mao Tai, but another white Chinese liquor that takes the top of your head off. That and beer are a lethal mixture. After a few toasts the table began to curl at the edges and the people to weave. It was an effort to concentrate. The fish arrived, signalling the end of the meal. It was a magnificent creature, steamed in ginger and garlic and decorated with radish flowers and green and red sweet peppers. The flesh literally slid off the bones, tender and succulent. Little sweet cakes and orange segments ended the feast.

Y— was on her feet again in front of the microphone. "The banquet is over," she announced. "Thank you for coming. Goodnight." Everybody rose and streamed toward the exit. I barely had time to thank my hosts. Chinese parties always end abruptly.

22 September 1988

DEAR WENDY,

Thank you for the care package. The shortbread particularly was a godsend. I keep it in my fridge, and nibble on it, and will be sad when it's all gone. The almonds I'm hoarding for a "special occasion" or when I need a lift.

22 September 1988

DEAR KURT,

You asked how this return to Paradise came about. Before I went home, I had a verbal invitation from the institute to develop and teach a tourism course for a year. However, it was a verbal invitation, and being the stickler for detail that I am, I did not take it as a commitment until I saw it in writing. I tried very hard to settle down, but could not be content. There was a terrible restlessness. Paradise spoiled me. As you know life is simple here. And if one is not gregarious, and can function without the frills of Western living, this is a perfect setting for writing. The months passed and nothing further was heard from the institute, and I began to think it was just one of those things. When in late June the written invitation arrived, I had more or less resigned myself to not coming back. I sat on the letter for a whole two weeks. My life was in a turmoil. "To go or not to go, that was the question." In the end the siren song of Paradise was too much, so here I am.

A week before I left, I sold my red 1980 Toyota Tercel. Genevieve was the first and only brand new car I had ever owned. I got her the day she came off the ship. She was beautiful, and if ever there was a machine I loved, it was that car. Last year, she sat in the driveway unused. It took a lot of cash to get her roadworthy again. The garage man was quite adamant when he said to me, "Don't leave her sitting another year."

It took a great deal of soul-searching to sell her. It was the end of an era. The day the new owner, a very nice young woman, drove off in her, I could have wept. In my mind the

simple act of selling a car took on a deeper significance. I
was closing a chapter of my life.

Other totally unrelated things were happening at the
same time. My sons are gradually leaving home. Soon the
castle by the sea will be almost empty. All this plagued me.
Still I could not resist the siren song of Paradise. It is in my
blood, and right or wrong, here I am until next July.

22 September 1988   In the six months I've been away, Beijing has changed in subtle ways. In the few times I've been
to town on the public bus, I actually sat. Last Sunday when
I went to the Forbidden City, the conductor, a jolly woman,
asked a young man to give me his seat, and insisted I take
it. She asked very politely where I was going, and made sure
I got off safely and at the right place. She even smiled and
waved goodbye! That really gave me pause. Am I that old
and decrepit? That evening I looked very carefully in the
bathroom mirror. There is a lot of grey hair, and crow's feet
about the eyes. The lines at the corners of the mouth are
visible even if I don't smile. But I'm not that old! So it can't
be me. It is Paradise changing.

25 September 1988   Happy Mid-Autumn Festival! Campus
is oddly quiet today. Sundays usually are, but it is particularly so today. Most of the population is probably nursing a
hangover.

After class W—, a moon-faced little girl with two stiff
pigtails who is the monitor of the junior class, ran after me.
"We are having a party this evening in the classroom. You
will come," she said earnestly, peering over the rims of her
spectacles.

I was still groping for a reply, when she ran off giggling.
My first instinct was not to go. I was still getting my sea-legs
on campus and did not feel I should be fraternizing with the
students. The administration's attitude in that regard has

been ambiguous to say the least. However, the other FEs did not have my scruples.

"You're being a snob," Marc pronounced. That galvanized me. I put on a jacket and tie, and went to the classroom at the appointed time.

The room had been transformed. Colored paper lanterns hung from streamers that crisscrossed the room. The desks were arranged in a large U, and white paper was tacked to the tabletops. Each place had a bowl, a pair of chopsticks wrapped in cellophane, a spoon, and a paper napkin. W— greeted me at the door. She had loosened her hair, and put on a red dress with puffed sleeves. As a matter of fact, all the girls were in dresses, looking very grown up. The boys were in suits. I was glad I was wearing a tie.

There was an amazing array of food cooked on one hot plate using one large pan. Each person contributed one dish and took turns cooking. There was a great deal of joshing. A vote was taken as to who is the best cook of them all. W— was the unanimous choice. Well, almost. G—, a young man who sat next to me, remarked sourly, "She is the monitor, and her father . . . " The rest was lost in the hubbub. And I was glad.

Afterwards I went to meet Marc in the pub in the foreign students' building for a pint and a post mortem. We were the only ones there! After a while the place was beginning to get on my nerves, and I wanted to leave, when Eric, a French student, stuck his head through the door and said there was a party upstairs, "just follow the noise." Oh, what the heck. We picked up a bottle of beer each and sauntered upstairs.

The noise was quite deafening. A ghetto-blaster was booming out the latest in rock. The DJ was a Japanese lad who did a superb imitation of Stevie Wonder. The dancing was frantic. The Japanese were the most energetic in a mechanical sort of way. The French exuded sensuality, and the Ruskies were boisterous. There was lots of vodka, and delicious Russian sardines and cheese. The chaperones were out in force. It was the first time I met any of them. Vladimir, the chief, is a tubby man with a big moustache and an even bigger grin. Tanya, his female counterpart, speaks fluent Chinese with a Russian accent. And my, did her eyes sparkle at the mention of Canada! Makes you wonder, doesn't it? Then along came Big Daddy. Ivan is the chaperone of the chaperones. A rolypoly with a shock of stiff white hair jutting out of the sides of his head, and the meanest, coldest eyes since Richard Widmark pushed the old lady down the stairs in *Kiss of Death*. Ivan was the party pooper. The Ruskies didn't stay long after he appeared. It is funny how the departure of one group takes the fizz out of things. Anyway it was time to stagger home. They lock the building at 11:00 P.M. pronto. One of the drawbacks of living in these sanitized surroundings.

2

▶

10 October 1988

My Dear Nicky,

Last night, the Canadian contingent—all three of us, plus the American wife of one—celebrated Thanksgiving. There was Veronica, who is built like a Caucasian Happy Buddha; Dick, a Torontonian married to Maisy, an American, who lived in Amityville, one block from the infamous house; and me. Veronica is the bubbly sort. Dick is dour and has a twitchy habit of fidgeting with his fly. I mentioned in another letter that he has the aura of a defrocked priest.

It was a "Canadian evening" except for the cuisine. There was no turkey. We would not be able to cook it even if one had been available. Although the kitchen is equipped with a gas oven, it is so small and the rack is so close to the top that the turkey would have to be very flat indeed to squeeze in. Instead we had spaghetti, a huge salad, and fruit. Bright yellow melons from Xinjiang and little green oranges from Yuanan which are a deep purplish red on the inside and very sweet are in season. The wine from Qingdao, with a label that read "White Dried Wine," was quite tasty. No, it does not come in cubes in spite of its odd name. The entertainment was Canadiana, ranging from Maureen Forester and the VSO, to Leonard Cohen, Tom Keenlyside, and a rock group called The Outlets, whom we know very well. It was a very pleasant evening.

Veronica has been away from Canada for seven or eight years, and is quite used to it. Dick and Maisy are terribly homesick, and weekly phone calls from home do not help

25

them settle down. I was filled with nostalgia thinking of the Thanksgiving dinner Russ and Wendy cooked for me before I left. Thanksgiving should be every day of our lives. I know I have a lot to be thankful for.

It has been a hectic week. The long weekend for National Day holidays seemed to throw everyone off course. The gigantic portraits of Lenin, Stalin, Marx, and Engels were trotted out onto Tiananmen Square. The vast Square was blanketed with flowers and shrubs all grown in flats. Portable fountains played. Two huge dragons made of shrubs and flowers with lasers cleverly concealed in their gaping maws stood on opposite sides of the Square. There was a huge panda waving a bouquet, and, of all things, a bull also clutching a bunch of flowers. Ferdinand, I presume.

The celebrations were severely cut back this year. There was no parade or fireworks. But the Forbidden City was lit up and the Great Hall of the People and the National Museum were outlined in lights. Laser beams crackled between the two giant dragons on the Square. The crowds were unbelievable but happy and friendly.

The Olympics is on everybody's mind. China did quite well I thought, although the press contends that they should have done much better. The country needs all the morale boosters it can get, for there are serious problems. The economic reforms are not doing well, and there are rumblings of arm-twisting in high places.

Sugar has disappeared from local stores. However, I managed to find a tiny bag in the Friendly Store the other day. People are stocking up on the most bizarre things. The papers reported a woman hoarded a thousand kilos of salt as a hedge against future shortage! Appliances like rice cookers, washing machines, and especially color TVs are in short supply. Good cigarettes are selling at ¥10 a packet. When you consider that the average income is ¥100 a month, and the average rent is ¥10, that is a shocking price.

There are long lines in front of banks. People are withdrawing their money. Last Wednesday the banks closed early because there was a run on cash. Still, people seem cheerful, and everything is calm.

14 October 1988

My Dear Mark,
Happy Birthday!

I am listening to Berlioz's *Harold in Italy* as I write this. I remember people, places, and events with music. Each of you has a musical theme. I bought *Harold in Italy* the day you were born, and it became your music. *Harold's* theme, which is for solo viola, and heard right from the beginning, became your theme. I used to hum it to you when you were a baby, and I rocked you back to sleep after the 2 A.M. bottle. That was a long time ago. But it seems like yesterday.

I am flipping through a scrapbook of memories in my mind. In the last year or so, I have often thought of a strange experience which I had many years ago. At that time I worked with a man called Jack McLaren, who I thought was eccentric. But he was a nice person and quite spiritual. One time he dragged me to a lecture by an Indian guru. The subject was astral projection. I knew nothing about it, and being interested in travel, facetiously thought it would be amusing. It could save a lot of airfares if it worked. I went on a lark, and the Indian guru did not dispel my skepticism. It sounded too pat. Nevertheless, I decided to try it. Nothing happened.

Then one night, weeks later, something did. Afterwards I could not be sure whether it was an out of body experience or just a very vivid dream. The strange experience, beautiful and terrifying left a cryptic phrase firmly imprinted on my mind. "Keep the flame . . . "

In the last ten years I've had occasion to ponder the meaning of the flame rather seriously. Particularly after the heart attacks. I realized then that the flame is the driving force of life. With me, it's writing. Coming to China was the first step toward realizing myself. Breaking away from home, family, a whole way of life, is painful. Who said it was going to be easy? But sacrifices have to be made if life is to be worthwhile. Teaching has brought new meaning into my life. And I have the time and energy to write in earnest. Doors have opened for me that I didn't know existed. A whole new life has begun.

Your flame is music. You found it young. Nurture it;

protect it and it will light your way through life . . .

15 October 1988   As I settle into my routine, and gradually attach names to faces in my rather large classes, a few students invariably stand out from the rest.

The first time I stood in front of my senior class, and the rows of faces seemed to stretch up to the rafters, my knees knocked together. I could feel the quiver in my voice when I said, "Good morning, ladies and gentlemen . . . " Silence. Seventy pairs of eyes were fixed on me. I repeated, "Good morning, ladies and gentlemen," willing them, daring them to return the greeting. There was an embarrassed shuffling, then a murmur. "Good morning . . . sir . . . teacher . . . " and laughter. The ice was broken. I wrote my name on the board. "You may called me by my given name, or you may address me as Mr. —. You can call me teacher, but you MAY NOT call me 'Sir '." Willie the slick operator spoke up. "We will call you by your name. It's more . . . " he looked around the classroom for the right word. Someone supplied, "informal," another said, "casual." "Friendly," growled a scruffy young man with greasy hair and beard, and the left lens of his spectacles taped together with a Band-Aid, from the middle of the room. The class rebel, I thought. I did not like the purple beret. I did not like the olive green sweater that was two sizes too big. The patched-up glasses gave me the willies. I did not like him.

I launched into the rules of the game. The class is too big for a roll call, I said. Besides, "You are young men and women; not children. And I will not treat you as children. Nobody is forced to come to class. However, if you don't, you will most likely fail." That caused a gasp or two. "You are expected to work very hard, because I have worked hard to develop this course." It was a speech that they did not expect from a foreigner. All through the first lecture the lad with the broken glasses stared straight at me. It was as though the words were written on my forehead. I looked away at the stylish girl in the front row; at the girl in the second row who was knitting; at Willie, who beamed blankly at me; at the thin young man next to him who hung his head and concentrated on the graffiti carved into his desk top; at the two girls in the back with their heads together, whispering; at a skinny girl who was all skin and bone, and enormous eyes, who was writing down every word I said; at the ruddy-cheeked young man on the far aisle with the bland expression but eyes that sparkled with intelligence; at the strange fellow slumped across his desk at the back of the room making strange gurgling sounds. But my gaze always came back to the young man with the broken glasses.

For the last half-hour, I asked the class to write a self-introduction.

Most of the paragraphs were stereotypical. But there were exceptions.

"I am a Party member. I want to work in tourism to make money for my country and get me a high position," wrote Willie.

"I want to work in tourism because it brings in foreign currency which my country needs . . . "

"I come from a very backward village. When I graduate I will go back there and do something uninteresting. There is no tourism in the village . . . "

"I come from the south where the young men are handsome and passionate. I hope I will get sent back there when I graduate. Northern men are chauvinists, crude and ugly . . ."

"I want to travel and meet foreigners who are kind . . . "

"Tourism is a way of going abroad. I want to see San Francisco and New York. But Hong Kong or Tokyo would be nice too . . . "

"If only I could be an electrician . . . "

"I don't want to be in this institute at all . . . " That took courage, I thought.

There were two that caught my attention:

"I am the only person in my family who has been to school. My brothers and sisters are illiterate. Although it is not easy for a farm boy to get this far, I don't want to be here. Actually I want to be a singer . . . " The name at the foot of the page was A—.

The bell rang. Everyone rushed from the room, for the students' canteen started serving lunch fifteen minutes earlier, and latecomers sometimes went without. The young man with the broken glasses took his time. When the last person had left he handed me his paper, bowed gravely and was gone.

"I don't know why I'm here . . . I want to be a writer . . . " he wrote. His name was J—.

The absentee rate is fairly high. The other FEs are already complaining that half their classes do not attend. In my large classes they are less conspicuous. But J— has not been seen in the last two weeks.

"What are the students who don't come to class doing?" I asked Willie, who purports to know everything as he walked me back to the apartment after class. He shrugged. "Sleep. They play mahjong all night . . . and drink . . . "

"But that's against the rules, isn't it?"

Willie grinned, and his eyes became tiny slits. "Nobody bothers about the rules around here." We were silent for awhile.

"Why do they do it?" I picked up the conversation again.

"Because they feel education is useless. They will graduate soon, and they will get assigned a job that they know they will hate. And that's the rest of their lives! So they're getting as much enjoyment as they can, while they can."

"Why are you different?"

Willie stopped grinning. He flicked the cowlick of hair out of his eyes and winked impishly at me. Willie knows his way around. He will be all right.

The other night I was coming out of the tuck shop when I collided with J—, the would-be writer, who was going in.

He looked sleazier then I remembered. His face was scratched and bruised. There was more tape on the broken lens of his glasses from which a few shards were missing. He looked comical and pathetic. "Why haven't you been to class?" He hung his head. "I was doing other things. But I promise to come from now on."

"The choice is yours," I said and started to walk away. He started after me.

"They say you're a writer," he said. "Can I come and talk

to you?"

"Certainly, you may," and I gave him my apartment and phone number.

"When?" there was a kind of urgency in his voice.

"Any time."

"Now?" That was not my intention. I had been looking forward to a hot bath, a cupcake, coffee, and a bit of brandy and Schubert lieder that evening.

He noticed my hesitation, and a cloud crossed his face. These young people are so brittle, and easily bruised. "I was just thinking we'll have to go back to the tuck shop for another cupcake. Do you like them?" He brightened instantly. "And I need cigarettes. You smoke, don't you?" We talked about books and writing until Uncle Panda phoned from the front desk to say he was locking up. The next day J— brought me a short story written in Chinese. I knew he did not believe I could read it. So I read a few pages aloud, although he had to decipher a few characters which his scrawl made hard to recognize.

"Phantoms" is the story of a boy who is left to be raised by his grandmother after his mother dies. Many years later the father, who has become a stranger, reclaims him, and takes him to live in another town. Cut off from the grandmother's warm, happy household, and his friends, the boy must learn to cope with the humorless and somewhat distant father. It is a tale of childhood fears told simply and honestly. It was obviously autobiographical and might have been mawkish. But there wasn't a hint of self-pity in it. It was the best thing I've read in a long while. I was impressed.

16 October 1988   J— has become a regular visitor. In a way, I am becoming dependent on his company. I look forward to these visits and I wish I had more books and music to share. He soaks up everything that comes his way. He has an endlessly curious mind which is already stuffed with Nietzsche, Freud, Jung, and Sartre; Maugham, Steinbeck, Faulkner, Hemingway and Lawrence—all read in Chinese translations. Strange bedfellows indeed for Marx and Engels and Mao. He has stopped cutting classes, though how he manages to read with those taped-up glasses I don't know. I have spoken to him about getting them fixed for safety's sake. Those slivers of glass look dangerous. He said he would but so far nothing has happened. Perhaps I should do something about it.

19 October 1988   Last night, J— phoned to ask if he could bring a friend to visit. I agreed. The friend turned out to be A—, the student who wanted to be a singer. I have not seen him in class for weeks, and he was shy and apprehensive until I explained that in the classroom I'm the teacher, out of it I am a friend. The two roles are distinct and separate, and we need not talk about studies unless he wanted to.

When A— talks about art and music his face lights up. There is a tremendous surge of excitement. His shaky English falters and evaporates. He continues in heavily accented Mandarin (or common speech as they call it). A— comes from a peasant family in the south. His parents, brothers, and sisters are all illiterate. That he has come this far is no small miracle. "Coming to university . . . to Beijing . . . was a dream come true," he said. But something was still missing from his life. He was lonely. He could not master common-speech. His coarse accent, which is still discernible, and the harsh, clipped southern rural speech pattern kept him at the bottom rung of campus social life. Most of the first two years he spent alone. Then he started rooming with J— and the two became close friends.

The day he found an abandoned acoustic guitar in a garbage dump was the turning point of his life. He cleaned it up, bought new strings, and started experimenting with it. Pretty soon he was playing, and writing songs. I haven't heard A— play or sing.

He had a trio going for a while: two guitars and drums. However, the drum set was vandalized and there is no money to replace it. So the trio died.

I played Mark's tape and Santana without any comment. Santana went over A—'s head. But The Outlets spoke to him. He listened, one foot tapping to the rhythm, and asked to hear the tape again when it stopped. The second time around he was humming along. I don't think he could grasp all the lyrics.

A— has an old young face. The deep lines at the corners of his mouth and eyes make him look much older than his twenty-one years. While the music played, the lines vanished and he was young and alive. Whatever troubles he had were forgotten. The hardest part of teaching in China is facing talented students who have been forced by family in A—'s case, and circumstances in J—'s, into courses where their talents are wasted. The worst of it is they cannot switch. I want to help but there is nothing I can do, except encourage and comfort. Even that has its limits. I will probably have to fail them both in the upcoming midterms because they have cut too many classes.

19 October 1988

My Dear Bunny,

This afternoon I went to the Lama Temple again.

I never thought I would see the day when the scaffolding would finally come off the great hall. I was anxious to see the great Buddha, but just being there again was enough. I wandered through all the other halls, putting off the moment to the very last.

Going up the marble steps I felt like a child on Christmas morning approaching the mysterious parcels under the tree. I pushed open the red lacquered door, and stepped into the cool, dim, incense-scented hall. The hall was deserted.

For a moment all I could make out were a few odd yellow shapes scattered around the floor. As my eyes adjusted to the gloom, I found the yellow objects seen so indistinctly were prayer cushions. I was standing at the foot of the great Buddha.

A red lacquered railing separated me from him. The

Buddha's toe was level with my chest. My eyes followed it to the bare ankles, then traced the lines of the robe that soared upward, sometimes visible and then lost in darkness. My gaze traveled ever upwards. Perhaps a cloud shifted. A ray of sunlight fell on a pair of hands, pressed palm to palm, the long graceful fingers gently curving backward. And still I probed the darkness. Then out of the gloom floated a pair of eyes, remote, serene with a hint of laughter in their depths. Those eyes seemed directed at me, and I could not tear myself away from them. Gradually the rest of the face came into focus. A smiling face; a face that has weathered many storms, endured, wept, and finally transcended all pain. The hall rose, tier upon tier of galleries. The huge pillars and the delicately carved railing, as fine as lace, were red lacquered. The ceilings and walls were a riot of green and blue shot through with gold. Four cleverly placed windows at the top let in the light. It was a stormy day of early autumn, when great thunderheads scud across the sky after rain, and the sunlight has a orangey gold tinge to it. I stood there for a long time, at peace with the world.

Six months ago, I left Beijing with a heavy heart. I felt I was leaving something unfinished. It was nothing I could lay a finger on. It was just a feeling. I went home and tried very hard to settle down, but I could not. I even took a job. But it did not help. I felt alien in my own house. Everything was strange. For example, I had even forgotten how to work my stereo, and I was never without music! It isn't that I have lost my love for music. Beethoven, Brahms, Mozart, and Mahler will always count among my dearest friends. It's just that I need music less. I have fewer material wants.

I have changed.

I long for simplicity and clarity; space in which to read, think, and write.

When I was a child, there was a scroll hanging in my father's study that I used to look at for long stretches at a time. There was a gazebo in the foreground, and an old man sitting in it, lost in thought, an open book on his knee. All around were gnarled pines, and craggy mountains that swept up into the clouds. That scroll filled me with a nameless longing. It was as though I had lost something, only did not know what it was, and so had no hope of ever finding it. The ache was there to remind me of the loss. I have not thought of that scroll until a moment ago. Now it hangs in my mind's eye as vividly as it did in my father's house. Now I contemplate it with the quiet joy of meeting an old friend. I have found the serenity I lacked. I have come home.

I feel more at home here than in "the castle by the sea." However, I have resisted making it too homey. I deliberately resist anything that smacks of permanence. I tell myself this is for one year only. I will work hard and enjoy it. And afterwards, I will go back to my other world. Either Beijing is enchanted, or it is a fever which I cannot shake—at least not yet. At the end of this year the school will have a tourism course in place and my work will be done. Then, perhaps, I will go away feeling "complete."

20 October 1988

MY DEAR DUCHESS,

I was delighted to hear from you. Your letter, together with my *China Daily,* was on my table in the dining hall at lunch.

The first breath of winter is rattling the windows. Before long it will be really cold.

Downtown, Chinese women walk around with pink long-johns showing under the hems of their skirts, and pink veils wrapped round their faces. With their noses in the air, they stride down the street dreaming they are Marlene Dietrich posing for von Sternberg. So if they walk into the occasional lamppost, it had no business being in the way. That's style, Duchess. Wrap your tiara in mothballs and bring your long-johns; wool socks and earmuffs too (the mink ones.)

Put away the sable and bring the old parka. In Beijing everybody looks like hell.

Bring lots of travelers cheques. U.S. is worth more, but you'll spend them just as quickly. And throat lozenges. 'Tis the season for Beijing throat. Don't plan on making your debut at Covent Garden within two months

The Last Emperor, which is showing in town (dubbed in Chinese) has created a huge interest in Pu Yi. Concurrently with the Bertolucci film, a Chinese serial in twenty-eight episodes is running on TV. The latter is quite spectacular. But Chinese bio-dramas leave no room for artistic license. And this one is no exception. It is ponderous. An FE of my acquaintance played the Peter O'Toole role. The powers-that-be are cashing in on the Pu Yi fad. Two of the young actors who played him as a child and teenager are tour guides in the Forbidden City, dressed in their costumes. There is also an exhibition of Pu Yi's regalia, and calligraphy by his brother, Pu Jie, considered one of the finest living calligraphers. Last week, we were shown yet another Chinese film variation on the theme of Pu Yi, called *The Last Empress*. It's the same story told from the point of view of Pu Yi's beautiful and headstrong wife, who becomes a dope addict and goes mad. A beautifully crafted film, but depressing. The surprising element in the film was the portrayal of Pu Yi's homosexuality. There is more openness now in many spheres.

Thank you for your offer to bring necessities. Actually, the only thing I am in dire need of is pipe tobacco.

I have marked your ladyship's visit on my diary. I was hoping you would have a day more or less open to speak to my class. But alas, Friday is the day I see the seniors, and that day you are on the Wall. And you mustn't miss that. Perhaps, if you could slink away from the hotel inspection, I could take you around Saturday. Beijing is full of nooks and corners that the turistas never see. In any case, we can certainly get together for a drink one of the evenings.

20 October 1989   I lunched at the Friendship Hotel. All my cronies are gone. However, the weirdos and the misfits were still hanging onto the bar and grousing and whining as before. I was glad that I was only visiting, and after a haircut beat a fast retreat to the sanity of these four walls.

24 October 1988

Dear Gregory,

Last weekend we went up to Chengde again.

This is the most beautiful part of the year. The air is sharp, foreshadowing the cold blast of winter that is not far behind. But the sun is warm, and the gold of the poplars and the red of maples blend with the brown earth lying fallow till the spring. Autumn is a special season. It is a time of transition; a milestone in the passage of time.

There were four of us: Marc who has "discovered" me, having alienated everyone else in the building. Their Eminences, Dick and Maisy; and I. A foreigner's tour for two days and three nights including transportation, accommodations, meals, and sightseeing costs over 900 FEC. The same tour for Chinese tourists costs 40 RMB!

Quite by chance I found a hole-in-the-wall travel agency at the south end of Tiananmen Square which would accept foreigners at Chinese prices. It took a bit of fast talking. The man in the kiosk was dubious about taking us. "Are the others all like you?" "No. They're the yellow-haired-blue-eyed variety." "The guides speak Chinese only." "I'll interpret." "The hotel . . . " the man made a face. "We'll rough it." I plunked the money down before he could change his mind.

Chengde is a place where I am inexplicably "at home." My mood lightens. The bright blue, green, and yellow tile, and the red walls makes my spirit soar. Tucked away in the mountains outside the Great Wall, it was once the summer retreat of the emperors, and a religious center. Kang Shi the conqueror, Yung Jung the usurper, and Qian Long the renaissance man all left their mark on the town, building a series of magnificent monasteries and palaces. The Pule Temple (or Temple of Universal Joy) is still a working temple, where lamas in bright red and yellow robes chant to the sound of drums, gongs, and trumpets that are capable of making one sustained but haunting note.

The hotel was a disaster. One huge room with rows of bunks like a barracks. The facilities were a joke. But the tour operator was kind, and for the lordly sum of 10 RMB each, upgraded us to the Guest House, where there were clean beds and bathrooms, though everything was damp and smelled of mildew.

We found a tiny restaurant that had room for only two tables. The only item on the menu was Mongolian hotpot. It was chilly after sundown and the hotpot hit the spot. While we ate, the delighted owner stood on the sidewalk shouting, "We have foreign guests!" And passers-by would stop in their tracks and gape at us.

Next morning Dick had a migraine and trailed about like a wet blanket, which caused Maisy's lip to curl in exasperation. Marc, who roomed with me, complained about my snoring, and went back to Beijing a day early. I enjoyed the trip but I'll not do another with this crew.

3

▶

1 November 1988   Once in a while, placid campus life
breaks out in wild exuberance. Halloween was celebrated
with a bacchanal to end them all. The jollity took place in the
pub and common room of the foreign students' building
across the street. Everybody chipped in for food and drink.
I had serious doubts about going, for it was a costume party,
which always puts me off. But there are a few people around
who have become my guardian angels, and have taken it
upon themselves to pry me loose from my computer from
time to time, so I went.

A weird collection of foreigners gathered in the foreign
students' building Halloween night. Curtains, bedspreads,
sheets, and towels were turned into costumes. Some were
quite elaborate. I wore my (genuine) Egyptian galabeya,
and a towel for a turban.

The Ruskies, who are usually quite dour, were the life of
the party, and the most boisterous. The two chaperones,
both middle-aged and portly, came in drag. A girl who
doesn't speak of word of English lip-synched "Memory" to
perfection. The French were plastered before the party began
and went from there. The Ruskies brought caviar, real vodka,
and delicious smoked sardines and cheese. Someone con-
cocted a huge salad, cold chicken, and ham. The *pe-jio*
flowed. And a bottle of Glen made a brief but very welcome
appearance. It was very quickly mayo'd.

Ninotchka, a buxom Russian, unrecognizable in black

silk and sequins, plied me with vodka and caviar on thin wafers. The music was so loud we had to shout in each other's ear. "You are from Japan?" she shouted in guttural Chinese. "Canada," I yelled back. "Much nicer," she beamed. "We dance," and proceeded to wheel me round the floor. My head was spinning. Everything whirled faster and faster. I kept trying to think, is this *glasnost* or *perestroika*? Or does it really matter?

The two born-again Christian American students and the Mormon huddled in a corner looking martyred. They are here to learn Chinese, and to spread the word by good example. They must have been waiting for the big foot to fall out of the sky any moment.

Campus parties shut down at eleven. All of God's children get locked into or out of their respective buildings. Halloween night was no exception. This morning we were a sad lot, creeping around campus. I did not have classes, but the ones that did were less than happy.

2 November 1988   I deliberately resisted buying kitchen utensils, etc., as I did not want to make this place too much like home.

One day I found a clay pot as I poked about the market-place across the street.

It was a very fine-looking pot, that kept screaming, "Buy me! Buy me!" And when the woman keeping the stall dropped the price from eight yuan to five yuan I bought it! It sat idle in the kitchen for a while, till Assistant Dean Z— saw it. Z— is a gourmet cook, and kept dropping unsubtle hints that I should try the pot. Finally he and his wife convinced me to get a few more things. One Sunday I went to town and bought a cleaver, spatula and some ladles. Then I got crockery enough for four, since I only have four chairs in the dining room.

I invited the Z—'s one evening for dessert. They came thinking I had cooked, and ooh'd and aahh'd over the cheesecake and the Black Forest torte. Then I had to tell them the clay pot remains idle and the cakes had come from the Beijing-Toronto Hotel.

It didn't take long for J— to discover the clay pot.

"We will have a party," he said, stretched out on the carpet, blowing smoke rings at the ceiling. He rattled on happily about the menu. "I only have four sets of eating utensils," I reminded him, "and one pot." "Never mind, we will bring everything," he said expansively. I was beginning to worry. "Look I'll pay for the food, but we have to keep the numbers down." "Of course. We'll have the best cooks." He named two girls, M— and W—, and a young man, G—. "And A—. He can cook one dish, but he does it well."

A few evenings later the entire group descended on me. They walked through the rooms, looked at everything, including the insides of closets. W— looked at the family photos on the bookcase. "Who are they?" she asked. "My sons." W— made the appropriate noises of consternation that I have grown sons. "I like them all," she said. "When will they come to China?" "I don't think they will," I said. W—pouted. After the apartment was inspected and found satisfactory, we settled on the following Saturday as a date.

G— decided my collection of tapes was "old fashioned" and volunteered to bring some of his. This created a small controversy. The two girls opined that G— has no ear for music. G— reddened. A— said he would bring his guitar. I gave them money for the food and they left chattering as merrily as a swarm of sparrows.

Saturday they arrived right on time. In one string basket was a live chicken. In another was a rabbit.

"Very fat, and juicy," M— pronounced. She had selected it herself. A fish swam in a pail of water. There were bags and bags of vegetables, and flour, and spices. I was dismayed at all the live things. The chicken and the fish did not particularly upset me. But the fluffy white rabbit with pink eyes!

The whole motley crew vanished into the kitchen. The door was shut, thank God. Still, I could hear the rattling of pots and dishes, the thumping of the cleaver on the cutting board. Presently the squawking of the chicken, and the high pitched squeal of the rabbit. I grabbed the first tape I could lay hands on, popped it into the ghetto-blaster, and turned up the volume.

A little later, M— came out of the kitchen smiling. She plunked herself into the armchair and took up her knitting. "Everything's fine," she said contentedly, and wrinkled her nose at the ghetto-blaster, "except that."

I took off Wagner and put on Sinatra. M—'s knitting needles clicked. "What are you making?" I asked. "A scarf." She held it up for me to see. "Who is it for?" She blushed and grinned impishly. "Someone I know?" The grin got wider. "He's in the kitchen," she said, being deliberately mysterious. I pretended I couldn't guess.

Wonderful smells were coming from the kitchen. M— put down her knitting and went back to the kitchen. From behind the closed door, I could hear her giving directions. The boys were demurring but M— would brook no non-sense. She is a natural homemaker. I wonder what she is doing here. The meal was incredible! G— brought a bottle of white lightning and before long was merrily drunk. After-wards the dishes vanished into the kitchen. I did not ques-tion. Finally everybody was relaxed. M— was ensconced in the armchair. G— was slumped in my desk chair. J— lay on the carpet. A— sat cross-legged beside him strumming his guitar and singing a Chinese pop song. W— was curled up in a corner of the sofa, looking snug. I went into the kitchen to make coffee. There was a moment of dread as the door swung open. I did not know what to expect. But the place was spotless. All the debris had been whisked away.

I told them they could cook here whenever they liked.

2 November 1988

Dear Robert,

Academe suits me to the extent that I'm becoming the absent-minded professor. This morning I rose at the usual hour, five-thirty, and went to meet the assistant dean for T'ai Chi. He is a cheerful little man. And I do mean little, for

I loom over him, but very kind and patient. I'm sure he rues the day he took me on as a pupil. I am all arms and legs, and no coordination to speak of. Turn around and I'm lost. Ninety minutes later, as the sun came over the horizon, I came back to my apartment, showered, had a leisurely breakfast of croissant, yogurt, fruit, and coffee accompanied by a Mendelssohn trio (the one in G Minor) and a bit of Mozart, and settled down to reread my lecture notes. At ten to ten, I walked across campus to my classroom and found it filled with strangers.

How dare they switch classrooms on me without notice!

I marched up to the office, smoke slowly seeping from ears and nostrils. The assistant dean was just coming down the stairs.

"What's the matter? They said you were ill." "Who did?" "Your students . . . " "My students?" "You didn't go to your eight o'clock class." I was totally deflated. It's Tuesday, and my class is at 8 A.M. and not 10 as on Thursday and Friday.

I am writing the textbook for the senior tourism course and teaching it at the same time. Twice a week, I meet the juniors for something called "Hotel English." This is an oral class, but, with fifty students, is less than effective. The plagiarized textbook, which was written for Finnish hotel workers dealing with English tourists, is absolutely irrelevant to China. Chinese students learn everything by rote. Thus they commit to memory such deathless lines as "The sauna opens at eleven," without the foggiest idea of what a sauna is. My own misadventures in a sauna in Helsinki brought peals of laughter and not a few red faces. Chinese students are real prudes.

My copy of the text is covered with great big crosses and circles, and angry margin notes. I have come to the conclusion that the only sensible way of teaching this text is to turn it upside down and inside out. For instance, in one exercise a woman asks a travel agent to book her a "cheap" hotel. She actually uses the word. The travel agent goes into rhapsodies describing a luxury resort. The woman balks at the price. Travel agent: "This is an expensive town. Shall I book it?"

This morning I had the class crossing out whole pages of dialogue again.

Lizzie, an intense young woman with thick glasses, had doubt written all over her sallow face. "Sir," she finally spoke up in a carefully cultivated American accent, "it can't be all wrong." "Believe me, it is," I replied. "But it's in the book," Lizzie insisted. Chinese students do not understand that books do not always contain truth. No wonder service is so marvelous in this country. But I'm having a lot of fun with this class.

The first breath of winter is rattling the windows. Across the way, the wooden scaffolding on the new six-story girls' dormitory swings and squeaks. The workmen dangle from it like spiders, with neither hard hats nor safety belts. Below, dust devils whirl like ghostly dervishes. But the sky is blue and brilliant, and the sunlight on my back is still warm. Before long it will be cold.

Nothing much is happening on the surface in the Middle Kingdom. The streets are jammed. But the hawk-eyed young men that go about whispering, "Change money?" out of the corners of their mouths are just a shade too desperate for my liking. Chinese brandy (all the best people drink it,) has gone from ¥5.40 to ¥8.70 a bottle. The average income is still around ¥100 a month. There are shortages but the grain ration is unchanged. Foreigners can still get what is not available in the open market at the good old Friendly Store. What would we do without it! We seem to be obsessed with food. Every Tuesday, Thursday, and Saturday afternoon a school bus takes us to the Friendly Store to shop. Thursday is the best because we get to go to the one in the diplomatic quarter where there is more variety (at higher prices, payable in FEC only). And after shopping there is a stop at the Holiday Inn Lido, where they serve real coffee and doughnuts.

Every day there are rumors of shortages. One nervous American colleague bought a case of toilet paper and urged everyone else to do the same. "My sources tell me there might not be any next week," he said importantly, "then you'll be s-o-r-r-y." Bill is an alarmist.

As the winter comes on there is every indication that there will be a general belt-tightening. Just where it will lead no one knows. But, as Candide put it, it's the best of all possible worlds.

5 November 1988   Marc called right after supper. "I know you're working. But we're all going over to the pub for a brew or two. See you there." The line went dead before I had a chance to get a word in sideways. I had been writing all day, and my brain was turning into mush. I was really tired once I stopped. One beer and it's bedtime, I told myself. I was moving about slowly, getting ready to leave when there was a knock at the door. I went to open it with my coat half on.

J— leaned against the jamb. "You're going out," he said. The disappointment was unmistakable. "I do go out from time to time." I let him in and shut the door. "I had to see you." J— slumped into a chair. He did not look well, but he said he was not ill. Just cold and tired. He had been missing classes again and midterms are around the corner.

I made coffee and we drank in silence. J— chain-smoked. There was something on his mind which he obviously wanted to tell me about, in his own time and in his own way. I waited.

"I belong to an arts group," he finally began.

There was a group of young painters who were disaffected by what they were taught at the Art Academy and decided to leave and strike out for themselves.

They banded together and formed a commune somewhere in the teeming heart of Beijing.

"It doesn't matter where they live. They have to move from time to time." "Because of the law?" J— shrugged. The commune is growing and now includes musicians and writers as well. A— became friendly with one of the painters, who had some unusual ideas about art as a performance. Where A— goes, J— is sure to follow. That is how he became involved with the group.

At first he enjoyed the company. The bohemian life-style was exciting. Their unorthodox views of art and life were fascinating. Most of all, it was a place where he could find kindred spirits; where he could talk about books and writing and art; where he could express himself freely without being censored. He began to spend a lot to time at the commune.

"That's where I go when I'm not in class," he confessed.

But now he was disillusioned. Most of these young artists do nothing but sit around smoking and drinking, and grousing about the drabness of their lives, waiting for inspiration to strike like a bolt of lightning that never comes. Even worse, they have begun to leech on J—. Since the beginning of term, J— has been giving a substantial part of his monthly allowance of 75 RMB to support the young artists, leaving himself short. He started borrowing from his classmates. A five here and a ten there, and the debt has reached 450 RMB. His creditors are after him to pay. With his back to wall, he has finally come to realize the fragility of the friendship of the young artists.

"My family is not badly off, but I can't ask my father again. He bailed me out once before." He looked at me helplessly. "I'm bad . . . " "Not bad," I said, "just confused and lonely." He buried his face in his hands and wept. Great sobs shook him. I was aghast. I was sure he could be heard in the corridor. I was suddenly paranoid about eavesdroppers. I put my arms around him to try and calm him, but that seemed to make it worse. I had horrible visions of someone bursting through the door. What would it look like?

Finally J—stopped crying. I made more coffee and added a dash of brandy. We were both shaking. J— was apologetic. "I don't know why I cried. I haven't done that since I was a kid . . . " "It's alright. You probably needed it." "I don't know whether I was crying for me . . . or . . . " He was probably thinking of A—. He wiped his nose with his hand and wiped his hand on his jeans in one swift movement ". . . or for all of us."

I was pacing the floor. He looked at me through his patched-up glasses, waiting.

I spoke rapidly in short, jerky sentences. I would help him pay off his debts and get a pair of glasses. But he would have to quit the artist group. He has a talent he must hone and discipline, and he must study and graduate, I finished gasping.

"Sooner or later, they all want something." Marc's voice was ringing in my mind. "Foreigners are a soft touch. We're far from home; we're alone; we're vulnerable." I knew all that. I've been in China longer than Marc. So why am I doing this?

J— must have sensed my doubt. He crossed the room, put his arms around me and laid his head on my shoulder like a weary child. There is an ingenuousness under the tough shell J— shows the world.

"You are more than a teacher, or even a friend. You are like a father," he broke into a tearful smile.

I warned him that I would not bail him out again, and would hold him to his half of the bargain.

When I got to the pub, all the others had gone except Marc, who was writing a letter.

"Well, doctor," he said without stopping his scribbling, "I didn't think you were coming." "Sorry." I sat down and poured myself a beer from the bottle on the table. "Student, huh?" I nodded. My hand was still shaking. Marc didn't miss a thing. "They're stupid; they're lazy; they're conniving little ingrates," Marc thumped the table with his fist. "So why are you putting yourself out?" The teacher of tough ghetto kids surfaces whenever he's been drinking. I let him ramble. I have a knack of tuning people out when they get tiresome. Marc doesn't know that yet. But he will find out.

7 November 1988   The attendance of the senior class has been quite satisfactory. There are a handful whom I refer to as "invisibles," who have been coming regularly now that midterm is drawing near. This is the time when my Chinese colleagues will drop subtle hints on what to expect. The less subtle actually divulge the questions. I have kept my paper close to my chest and only gave it to the office for typing at the last possible moment.

During a lull in class, a hand suddenly shot up. I recognized a smartly dressed girl with close cropped hair. C— is a gamin who speaks with an American accent.

"Teacher, can you tell us about the exam?" "I have already announced the time and the place. Be there." "Will we get good marks?" "That depends on you." C— is one of the invisibles who have deigned to appear in our midst. "Will we fail?" the girl persisted. "Yes, if you deserve to." A murmur ran around the room. Failing an exam is unheard of. "But teacher, if we fail you will lose face." C— was playing her trump card. "Wrong. If you fail, you lose face. A foreigner doesn't give a damn about face."

The "invisibles" I have encountered so far are all smart, well dressed, and speak good English. According to Willie, most of them work fulltime as guides. A few are in business for themselves, selling everything from chemical fertilizer to jeans.

The bell rang and everybody streamed from the room. I was gathering up my papers when a young "invisible" came up to me, and just stood grinning. "What can I do for you?" I asked, peering over the tops of my glasses.

He laughed. "You didn't recognize me!"

It was J—. His hair was cut short and neatly combed. The beard was gone.

He sported a pair of new horn-rimmed glasses which made him look very scholarly. The purple beret and the green sweater were also missing. He laughed happily at my surprise, obviously delighted with his new image. I laughed too.

He walked me back to the apartment. "I want to invite you to dinner. I want to celebrate the beginning of the rest of my life." I agreed on condition that he does not overspend.

We went to a little dumpling restaurant on the north road, not far from campus, which is always crowded with ditch-diggers, bricklayers, and muleteers. We had a plate of squid cooked in a savory sauce of garlic and black beans, and a plate of eels, and mounds of dumplings.

Halfway through the meal, Marc and some Americans came in, saw me, and waved across the room. Marc made a questioning face at me before he sat down. He did not recognize who I was eating with.

11 November 1988

DEAR RUSS & WENDY,

The Valkyries are bouncing off the walls of my living room/study. The pandemonium of Wagner's music matches the havoc in the room. I am surrounded by paper strewn across the floor, covered with violent red slashes. The aftermath of midterms is waiting to be wafted off to Valhalla. Actually, the results are quite gratifying. The spoken English of students here is several notches above those I had at the university last year, but their writing skills leave much to be desired. I'm glad I don't teach English.

After two months I am attaching names to faces. I have the usual spate of uncommon names: Juno, Athena, Abraham, Salome, and Stallone. A pretty girl calls herself Arthur, and Nell is a strapping boy with shoulders like a quarterback. I asked if it should be N-e-i-l. "No," said he, "it's N-e-l-l." What can I say?

Thursday I gave an oral exam to the junior class of fifty whom I have for "Hotel English." It was the longest day I've had in a long while. The exam started at 2:00 P.M., we broke for supper and resumed at 6:30 P.M.

It was the first really cold day, but the heat does not come on till next week. By 10:30 P.M. when the last student left the room I was stiff with cold. Though I was bundled to the eyeballs, my feet felt frozen to the bare cement floor. The door opened and in bounced someone I had never seen before.

"Who are you?" I asked. "I'm Jesus," he said settling in the chair across from me. "I'm your student." Jesus! I did not have him on my list and I had never seen him before. At the end of an exhausting day, I did not need to see Jesus!

Jesus turned out to be an auditor, and I was not about to give him the exam. I was through the ceiling like a rocket. Get out of my life, Jesus! I'm going home!

It took a couple of belts of Chinese brandy and a hot bath to get the chill out of my bones before I could get to sleep.

As it gets colder, this may be China's winter of discontent.

On the surface all is calm and all is bright. But the economy is in trouble. Somewhere behind closed doors a fierce struggle is going on. Judging by what is visible, Li Peng, the hardliner, is in the driver's seat. Zhao looks haggard whenever he appears on the news. Deng has been more visible than before, but looks like a fragile gnome.

The papers are full of stories of corruption. FEC is exchanging one-to-two for RMB. The government's silence amounts to a tacit admission that FEC is worth at least 50 percent more than the official currency. People are drawing their money out of banks and turning it into TVs and fridges. Wangfujing, the main shopping street, is a continuous stream of humanity. There is a shortage of washing machines, and purchases are limited to one per household. Sugar disappeared from grocery stores some time ago. Now salt is hard to come by, as shopkeepers withhold it to drive up the price. There are hints that there may be a shortage of grain as well. The harvest has been poor because of an exceptionally long winter followed by drought. But the fact is, the farmers are abandoning the land and coming into the cities to seek their fortunes. However, the jobs on building sites are drying up as project after project is shut down in a general belt-tightening. As it grows colder, these bewildered farmers huddle with their pathetic bundles under overpasses and around the air ducts of large buildings looking desperate. Although the vagrants are rounded up and sent home, they keep coming back. One old man has been sent back sixty-four times! Street crime is happening with increasing violence.

This week many enterprises that were not making money have been abruptly closed down. Retired cadres who have gone into business have been told to quit immediately or lose their pensions. This may well be the end of the Foreign Expert system too.

It is cabbage season. Every day the highways in front and behind the campus are clogged with lorries piled high with cabbages. It is a twenty kilometer traffic jam to the nearest depot a block from the Friendly Store. *China Daily* reports that 300 million kilograms are distributed per day. Walls and pyramids of cabbage are everywhere. Even on campus. Cabbage has a peculiar stink, and the air is heavy with it.

Living on campus I feel closer to the grassroots and not quite as cut off as the artificial environment that was the Friendly Zoo. These are interesting times we live in. Monty Python's big foot hovers over the country.

18 November 1988   I celebrated the end of midterms tonight at the Beijing Concert Hall. The Salzburg Chamber Orchestra, a group of fourteen young musicians, played a program of Mozart and Shostakovich. Their conductor, whose name escapes me, was a comical old man who shambled on stage like a walrus in evening dress, and flayed the air with long rubbery arms in a way that seemed to have no connection with the music. But the playing was superb.

I invited J— who had never been to a symphonic concert before. He has been working very hard the last few weeks. What is more he passed the midterm, which was a pleasant surprise. Thus it was a celebration for him too.

J— is a new man since he broke away from the commune of young artists. He has a positive outlook on his studies and his life. Most of all he believes in his own abilities as a writer of the future.

After the concert he invited me to his dormitory for tea. He shares a tiny room with five others, including A—. He has made ingenious use of the narrow bunk that is his living space. Three sides of the bunk are lines with shelves crammed with books. Hugo, Maugham, Nietzsche, Sartre, Faulkner, Steinbeck, Hemingway, Shakespeare—all in Chinese translations. In a corner he has rigged a desk just wide enough to write on, with a small reading light. We sat cross-legged on the bunk, with mugs of hot tea between us and talked about Mozart and Salzburg. J— has a very keen mind, and is starved for knowledge.

"There is so much to learn!" he exclaimed. "I'm just finding it out!"

Marc questioned me at length about J—'s transformation. I could give no satisfactory answer. Perhaps not being a trained teacher has its advantages.

I am not hampered by preconceived ideas, and therefore, have to rely on instinct, trial and error. Having one student like J— makes this whole experience worthwhile.

25 December 1988

MY DEAR MARK & NICKY,

Merry Christmas. It's still Christmas Eve at home. About now you should be having your Christmas dinner at Russ and Wendy's new home.

Thank you for the Christmas parcel which arrived a few days ago. I saved it to open this morning. I am savoring my favorite pipe tobacco, and nibbling on Swiss chocolate. *The Nutcracker Suite* is playing on the ghetto-blaster, and all is right with the world. I'm sitting here in the quiet morning. The sun is pouring in, though it is freezing cold outside. I am tired.

I have just finished one book, and planning the next. There is no end of things to do which makes these quiet moments all the more precious. This is my second Christmas away from home. I wonder where I shall be this time next year. At times 1988 feels like a runaway roller coaster. But it has been stimulating, and I have never felt more alive!

There was no caroling on Tiananmen Square this year. There is no cohesiveness in this group of FEs. Besides, it is a bit far.

The school authorities let us have the dining hall for a soirée and we did not have to shut down at eleven o'clock.

But we had to provide the food and drink ourselves. Chinese students were strictly not allowed. However, the foreign students were.

Preparations for the soirée was the main topic of conversation around the building for the last weeks. Everybody was expected to pitch in for a potluck dinner. I thought I would get away with a cake from the Beijing-Toronto Hotel, but that was not to be. Veronica, who was in charge of catering, cornered me in the corridor. She fills the corridor so there was no escape. "Marc says you do a m-eea-n curry." Her eyes sparkled. "And we do need hot food." Veronica has a smile that makes you go soft inside. So I was committed to making curry.

I was too busy to get involved in any of the sundry committees. There were all sorts of squabbles. Everybody was trying to reproduce their own Christmas past. As no two people have the same ideas, there were constant clashes. Marc held numerous meetings regarding the music, which he was responsible for. Everyone had a favorite carol, and a pet peeve. That people will actually quarrel over which carol should be played surely gives you a hint about some of the specimens here. A few days ago, the administration bought us a huge tree. It was actually too tall for the room. Nobody thought of chopping a bit off the bottom. Instead it went up bent over at the top. It took the *foos* * all day to get the lights to work. Finally it stood looking quite beautiful with all the baubles and things on it, in spite of the drooping star.

Yesterday morning the Russian students went into town and brought back another tree, a gift from the Soviet embassy. They must have been as busy as beavers the rest of the day, making ornaments. I must say they were inventive, sewing tiny animals out of colored cloth; folding paper and tin foil and even using dough colored with food dyes. The tree was the centerpiece of the dining hall and was a real success.

About eight o'clock people started drifting in with the

---

*From Chinese *fu wu yuen*, or "attendant." A bilingual word play.

starters. The Japanese students made sushi and tempura, the Ruskies did some fantastic things with fish and beef tartar. Someone made barbecued short ribs. Then about nine o'clock, the main dishes were brought in. There were a dozen salads; quite a few hot vegetables, roast chickens, canellone, and my curry. The French students made the desserts: crepes, fruit jellies, and several cakes. The first glass of Chinese wine is an assault on the digestive and the nervous systems. Afterwards it became quite acceptable. In fact, it seemed to improve as the evening wore on.

Fat and jolly Mr. Wang of the Foreign Affairs Bureau, guardian angel of FEs, arrived as Santa Claus, and distributed presents. A chorus of Japanese students sang "Silent Night" in English, Chinese, and Japanese. The American students, all three of them, did "Hark, the Herald Angels Sing." Then one of the Ruskies appeared as a Russian Santa, accompanied by Mrs. S. Santa wore a tall bearskin hat and a long, ankle length robe of wine-red velvet trimmed in white fur. Mrs. Santa had long golden braids, and a three-cornered hat trimmed with feathers. Her entire costume was white with gold trimming, down to the knee-high boots. They sang a lively song called "Kalinka" which is about snow-flakes, as one of the supervisors tried to explain in a mixture of English and Chinese.

Dancing and serious drinking was next on the agenda. Marc had taped all the music, but the Japanese students brought some tapes too, and had the temerity to put them on without permission. Marc is a morose and ill-tempered drunk, and there was nearly a fist-fight with the offender. The Japanese teachers swooped around the two. There was much bowing and hissing through clenched teeth. As usual, Marc overreacted and will eat crow the next few days. The jollity lasted way past midnight. The dancing ended with a Beatles song, "Back in the USSR." The Ruskies really kicked up their heels for that one, shouting, "Back in the US . . . back in the US . . . back in the USSR!"

When I toddled home, the phone was ringing off the hook. I picked it up. There was a giggle, then voices broke into "Silent Night." Somewhere in the middle the words got scrambled, and abruptly changed from English into Chinese. But everybody finished together. It was my students. A really thoughtful gesture.

25 December 1988

Dear Russ & Wendy,
Merry Christmas!

Thank you for the lovely card, and the gloves which arrived yesterday. The gloves fit perfectly, and are just what I need. The Chinese make presentable ladies' gloves but the ones for men are impossible. If only they would leave off the awful slogans, like "Rambo" in bold white letters across the knuckles!

The Canadian Ambassador and his wife hosted a dinner for the expatriates last Saturday. Out of three Canadians on campus, I was the only one invited. That caused a bit of a stir.

Her Eminence Maisy was incensed. Though she is not a Canadian, her husband is. Besides, she is a Lansky from Duluth! In fact, she stormed the Embassy demanding an invitation! Days went by and no invitation arrived. Each day at lunch Maisy would eagerly sort her mail and curl her lip at me across the table. "Still no invitation." Dick beside her twitches uncomfortably, his face slowly turning beet red. Marc kicks me under the table and whispers out of the corner of his mouth, "His balls are in the duck-press again." And sure enough the litany follows: if Dick weren't so shiftless, he'd demand his rights as a Canadian citizen. "You know how much it means to me," she sniffed. "Being stuck in this Aaa-w-ful place at Christmas!" Then, abruptly, "How could they miss us?" "It's nothing personal. The invitations were probably spewed out by a computer," Veronica tried to comfort, and put her foot in it instead. "Did you get your invitation?" Maisy demanded. "No. But I didn't get one last year either." "That's it," Maisy said triumphantly. "And you didn't do anything about it! Well, I'll demand an invitation in your name as well." Veronica groaned.

Their Eminences never got that invitation. But you get the drift of how people's perceptions are scrambled in

Paradise.

It was the usual "cast of thousands" affair. There were a few faces I recognized from last year. What passed for conversation was all gush and no substance. There was a mind-boggling spread: joints of beef, hams, and so on. The turkeys disappeared as quickly as they were put out. But for me the piece de resistance was the cold poached salmon. The booze flowed and flowed and flowed. A bottle of Glen made a brief but memorable appearance before it was consigned to the Land of *Mayo*. And I floated home happily sloshed.

1 January 1989   There were no banging pots and pans or firecrackers at midnight. Even the foreign students who live in the next building were silent. Vladimir, the guardian angel of the Russian students, and some of his flock went into a vacant lot outside the campus with a bundle of firecrackers. Vladimir had a "Double-Barrel," a wicked looking thing about a foot long, shaped like an hourglass. It gives two bangs. The first is a small "ping," then comes the big B-O-O-M !

You hold it between two fingers, at its narrowest point, light it, and toss. Vladimir held the firecracker firmly in his hand and was slow to throw. It went off in his hand, singeing his eyebrows and burning his hand. He is looking rather sheepish with no eyebrows and a blackened hand. Vladimir is a good sort, though. He tells everyone he sells furniture in Moscow. Probably with hollow legs.

21 January 1989

DEAR BUNNIE,
. . . This time last year I was on my way home, wandering Europe like a lost soul, stuck in the twilight zone between two worlds. As I sit here within the quiet of these four walls, I am peaceful and content. The dark red sofa and the match-

ing armchair beside the reading lamp; the poster of Manet's Venice which Nicky sent me a Christmas ago; your bust of Beethoven glaring from the bookcase—he too has come back to China. It is a simple apartment, but warm and comfortable and all I need. This is the place I live and work in. This is home.

Living on campus has put me in closer contact with the students. A small circle has formed around me. I finally bought a few kitchen utensils, and usually one or two will come by for Sunday dinner. The conversations are far-ranging, and often quite thought provoking. Inevitably I have become a father figure and confidante. That is gratifying, and humbling too. J—, who is a very promising writer, spends a great deal of time with me. If I am working or writing he will quietly read or write on the dining room table until I am finished. He also looks after me. Yesterday afternoon I gave an oral exam to my class of fifty juniors. It ran from 2:30 to almost 6 P.M. Halfway through the afternoon, J— quietly tiptoed in with a mug of hot tea and left again. When it was finally over, I turned off the light and locked the classroom. J— was sitting on the cold cement floor in the corridor waiting. "I just wanted to be sure you didn't need anything, " he said.

What version of Mr. Chips am I turning into?

4

▶

DEAR AL & IRENE,

Happy New Year! It is a cold grey day that threatens snow, and most people are still getting over last week's festivities. I am glad enough for the quietness; peace that I am loath to disturb except with music turned so low that it is barely perceptible.

1988 was an exciting year. In the short span I was home, Russel and Wendy married, and Nicky graduated. Those were milestones in my life.

It was not without a great deal of soul-searching, and many sleepless nights, that I decided to chuck everything and come back to China. I don't think anyone except my sons understand my need to be here. Nor is there much point trying to explain changing my life completely at 54. Coming to China has been the turning point of my life. Doors opened mysteriously. I have wanted to write since I was a child. Now I am writing as fast as I can, teaching, and still struggling with my endless novel on Qinshihuang.

This second year of teaching is easier than the first, but much more challenging. I am creating the tourism course as I teach it. The trouble is it takes longer to write the material than to teach it, and I am forever chasing myself.

A few weeks ago I went to Shanhaiguan for the weekend mainly to be by the sea again. It was very cold, and the salt-laden air reminded me of home, and how far away I am. I miss my home. I miss my sons. I could miss a thousand little things if I allowed myself the luxury. My foreign colleagues constantly grouse about one thing and another. They seem to forget that we are all here by choice. I am content.

Living on campus puts me in closer contact with the students than last year. There is seldom an evening when one student or another is not here. Most of them come from other cities, and miss their homes. For a few I have become a father figure. The majority will go back to their home-towns when they graduate in the summer. Those who have developed serious romantic attachments are anxious about the future of their relationships. Particularly if they are not from the same town. There will be many broken hearts in July. Looking at these young people with no control at all over their lives economically or socially, I am grateful that my sons were educated in Canada, and live there. It is exceedingly hard to be young and Chinese.

14 January 1989

DEAR KATHY,

This has been a hectic week. There is a conference of travel managers from across China on campus. A few weeks ago the dean invited me to read a paper at the conference. He is a pleasant man, a former army drill sergeant, with little education, and does not speak English. The native academics despise him, but he and I have hit it off well. I accepted.

It was days later before I thought to ask what language I was expected to use. "Chinese, of course," said he. "Most of the people will be non-English speaking." I balked. There is no way I could do it in Chinese. I'm bilingual, but not used to giving formal lectures in Chinese. "We'll get you an interpreter." The dean was not going to let me off the hook.

After thinking about it for a few days, I began to like the idea. The ham in me was surfacing. I decided to select an interpreter from among my students instead of using the young teacher who was recommended. The dean liked the idea. I asked for volunteers, and two boys and two girls showed up for "auditions." C— was good but moody and unpredictable. A prima donna I do not need. She quickly vanished from the scene. M— was prettier and more articulate. Willie was as sharp as a whip. J— has the best command of language among the three. It was very hard to single one out. I ruminated for several days and finally hit on the idea of using three interpreters instead of one. The dean was ecstatic. It would be good exposure for the students as well as the institute.

Each of the three was given a third of my paper which they translated into Chinese. Then the grueling part began. For several weeks, we worked very hard. I would read a few sentences and the interpreter would translate. I have always found it difficult to read off a script, even one I had written. Sooner or later, I drift into ad-libbing. The chemistry was right from the beginning. Also the three were with me eight hours a week, and were familiar with my idiosyncracies. It went off very well.

Judging from the general tone of the conference, the tourism industry is finally waking up to the fact that "all is not well in Paradise." They asked some pointed questions on how foreigners view travel in China, and I gave them the unvarnished truth, though expressed with humor. They laughed but the message sank in.

23 January 1989

DEAR DON,

It has been snowing steadily for the last two days, and the students have turned into small children again.

On Friday I walked into my senior class, and found the entire group of seventy assembled. There was mischief in the air. Y—, a pleasant farm boy from the far west, who is too shy to speak, grinned his greeting from across the room. But the grin was wider than usual. He was clutching a snowball. I made a gesture as if to catch, and he threw. I caught and tossed it back. Other missiles came flying then. I picked them up and tossed them back. It was a hoot! The room was a trifle damp afterwards, but the class went on. Last year I would not have done it. I am more relaxed, and the students here are more responsive. Although work never seems to end, I am enjoying my year. Living on campus has put me in closer contact with students. A group has formed around me, which is perhaps inevitable. Shades of Mr. Chips! But I assure you Captain Bligh still walks the deck and they know it.

Christmas was celebrated in the building with a suitable amount of jollity.

When New Year's rolled around, everyone seemed to sink into a grey lethargy. I roasted a chicken in my tiny gas oven. Chinese-built appliances often look better than they work. This time I was pleasantly surprised, though the chicken had to lie on its side or it would not fit. I had a bottle of very acceptable Chinese cabernet, and a bottle of Glenleven which was a Christmas present to myself. And that completed the menu. A student, J—, who is a very promising young writer, and his puppy, shared the dinner.

Earlier in the afternoon, when J— phoned to ask if he could bring his puppy, I said "yes" without thinking. I was anxiously hovering over the chicken at the time. It was my first experiment with the oven.

Later I wondered whether I heard right. Where would J— get a puppy? Surely he was bringing a classmate. I set an extra place at the table.

J— arrived wearing a voluminous coat. A tiny face peered out from under his collar. It was a puppy!

The puppy is an illegal resident, as pets are strictly verboten.

J— found the little thing wandering the corridors of the dormitory and took it in. He knew nothing about puppies. As a matter of fact, he never had a pet in his life. It was quite clear that the small animal and the young man were already attached to one another. "I call him Toto," J— said. I laughed. "Isn't it a good name?" J— asked. It was clear he had never heard of the Wizard of Oz, and it would take too long to explain. "It's a very good name," I assured him.

The puppy must have been newly weaned. It still wobbled on its legs, but it has huge paws, so it will probably be big one day. J— has made a bed for Toto out of a cardboard carton lined with an old discarded sweater. "The green hippie one you disliked," J— wagged a finger at me. "Did I dislike it?" "Of course you did!" "Did I say so?" "You didn't have to," J— grinned. "But it came in useful."

Toto shared the chicken and some vegetables. The little thing made himself quite at home, going from one room to the other, exploring. I had to whisk the tangle of computer wires out of his way, or he'd've fried himself chewing them.

Of course it had an accident or two. But having the little chap romp around the apartment, chewing the newspaper, and dragging my shoes was delightful. One appreciates simple pleasures living in China.

Promptly at eleven the phone rang. Uncle Panda's voice was loud and clear on the other end of the line. It was his bedtime and my guest has to leave. I protested it was New Year's Eve and I wanted to see in the New Year with my friend. But the Panda was adamant. "He's here nearly every day," he said. "He can visit tomorrow." That's China!

Glenleven gave me a pleasant glow, and Beethoven's Ninth on the ghetto-blaster heralded in the new year.

Away from academe, the reforms are stumbling along. Inflation is serious. There are shortages. There are cutbacks everywhere. Now there is concern whether the marketplace will be able to absorb all the graduates that the various schools will be turning out in a few months.

In another two years, graduates from universities will no longer be assigned jobs. They will have to find their own. No one in the country has had to look for a job in the last two generations, and no one has any idea how it's done. Not so long ago, the dean of Economics, who is a friend, invited me to give the talk on job-seeking. I accepted. A poster that read "HOW TO SELL YOURSELF" went up on the bulletin boards around campus announcing the event. The dean is one of those rare men around campus that has a sense of humor. But the very straightlaced administration was perturbed. What is that foreigner doing? The poor dean was called on the carpet to explain. The poster was a great gimmick. The talk had to be moved from the largest lecture room into the auditorium, and it was packed. The administration came too. I am a bit of a ham, I think. Between you, me, and the doorpost, I enjoyed the applause.

Young people feel terribly threatened. Many have frittered away four years at college, and are not prepared for life. With no real skills to sustain them, they find solace in all-night gambling and romance.

There was a near tragedy on campus just before Christmas.

A very pretty girl from Yunnan and a lad from Hubei had been dating since first year. Both will graduate in May. The relationship has gone well beyond "holding hands at the movies." The boy, aware that each would be sent back to the hometown, and that the relationship was doomed, tried to break off the romance. The girl objected. When tears and tantrums failed, she hired thugs from a village nearby to teach the boy a lesson. Three young hooligans armed with knives got into the grounds, and found the boy at the Saturday night dance. There was a brawl. The boy was cut, but the security guards swooped down in the nick of time. One young thug was caught on the spot. The other two were apprehended several hours later. All three are in jail. The odd thing is that there were no repercussions—so far—for either the girl or the boy. One theory is that both are due to graduate, and the school prefers to sweep the incident out the door with them.

There was a drama festival last month. I went to several events. I did not think it possible to do *A Streetcar Named Desire* in Chinese, and was astounded by the production. The Blanche was a tour de force. The Stanley was suitably beefy, and even bellowed "STELLA!" at the end of the first act with conviction. But he did not have the animal magnetism that the role requires. He was just an awkward hunk.

The next night I went to O'Neill's *The Emperor Jones*. This was the best of three offerings I saw. The play was done in a surrealistic style. The stage was dominated by a huge web and a spider played by a woman in white body-suit. It was almost a ballet. There was a considerable amount of dance done to African chants and drums. The internalized dialogue was spoken by off-stage voices. The actor who played Jones was magnificent. He should have played Stanley.

The third play was *Caine Mutiny Court Martial,* directed by Charlton Heston. This was another play I didn't think would work in Chinese. Queeg was played by a Humphrey Bogart look-alike complete with raspy lisp and baggy eyes.

I am more relaxed about going out at night now, but I still have to keep one eye on the time. If I miss the last bus, I'm sunk. That's the main drawback of "a country residence." My year in China is half gone again. I do not know what I will do next. I ought to try to settle down in Canada I suppose. But there is no longer an "anchor" there. I've learnt a lot about myself. I'm not as stiff-necked and starchy as I used to be. Am I a better man for it? I wish I knew.

25 January 1989   As I thought, "Phantoms" was entirely autobiographical. J— speaks of his family wistfully. The father, a mathematician who survived the Cultural Revolution, is a dour man who tends to reduce everything in life to a mathematical equation. The stepmother, who is a physician, is kind in a disinterested way. J— is very fond of a younger brother, who is going through the difficult late-teens.

Having Toto has changed J—'s life. In a way, the young man and dog have a lot in common. Both were left motherless at an early age, and both had to learn to cope more or less on their own. Toto has given J— an emotional focus. He has never been responsible for another living creature. Now the little dog has filled the void.

Every evening just after dark, J— phones. "Do you want to go for a walk?" I don my coat and together we head for the running track. J— carries Toto under his coat and lets him loose when we reach the track. He has taught the little chap to heel and to wait, and to go into the scruffy grass beside the track when anyone approaches. Toto understands. Some people in the building probably think I'm acting strangely these days. I go in to dinner late, order two dinners, but only eat one, or sometimes a bit of each, and take the rest away.

Dorothy Howard, who shared a table with me one evening, looked on with interest. When I started scraping the leftovers into a bowl I brought with me, she suddenly reached over and caught my wrist. I could tell her practiced nurse's fingers were searching for a pulse. I let her. "Are you all right?" she asked. "You tell me," I countered. "I think I'm fine." "I think you're working too hard. There's too much going on in your mind." I assured her I would try to relax. I finished scraping up the food. "Why do you do that?" Dorothy was curious. "Breakfast." I said getting up from the table.

The food was for Toto the next day.

27 January 1989   This evening J— appeared on the doorstep without Toto. He was sporting a long red scarf and a grin from ear to ear.

M—, who had knitted the scarf, was looking after Toto for the week. "He will get a lot more attention in the girls' dorm," said J—, fingering the thick wool scarf.

We talked about Napoleon's letters to Josephine which he had been reading. I am beginning to understand J—'s sudden interest in love letters. "I'm twenty-two and this is the first time I've felt this way about a girl." The brandy was relaxing him. "M—, M—, M—," he murmured under his breath. Then abruptly. "It doesn't sound right. I think I'll ask her to change it to Josephine." "And your own to Napoleon. You could be called Nap for short." We laughed.

Before he left, J— asked me to look after Toto for the duration of the spring break while he went home. I said I would think about it. Pets are not allowed in this building either. Toto is housebroken, and quiet. I suppose if I told the cleaning lady to take a few weeks off and cooked my own meals and greased a few palms . . .

27 January 1989

Dearest Mum,

The semester is over. The campus feels very empty, and after the hurly-burly of the term I am restless. The sun is brilliant but without warmth and the wind has a nasty cutting edge. I went for a brisk walk around the campus and up to the playing fields and back without meeting a soul. The library was the only place where there was any sign of life. Even the tuck shop was deserted. I bought some cake and yogurt, and came home and made myself a pot of hot tea to thaw out. It is cold! But the apartment is comfortable. We have the whole of February off for Spring Festival. They don't call it Chinese New Year anymore.

I am very tired. Perhaps that is why I feel the let-down so sharply at the end of term. The exams are over, and the marks, good, bad, and indifferent, are all in. The unaccustomed leisure is oppressing. Not that I have nothing to do, mind you. I have just started writing a new book; there is still the text that I will teach next semester; and an article to dash off for a magazine. But I just don't feel like any of it right now. Actually I want to be lazy for a while.

I was the last to finish exams. All the others who live in the building have gone off traveling. There are only a few Japanese teachers and me left. The Japanese always smile and bow, but they keep to themselves. There are enough of them to keep each other company. I am the odd man out in this building. Being equally fluent in English and Chinese has advantages and disadvantages. The Chinese don't know what to make of me, and neither do the foreigners.

Nearly every Saturday morning we go downtown to shop for food. Afterwards I stop at the Beijing-Toronto Hotel for (real) coffee, and sometimes a slice of apple pie topped with a dollop of ice-cream. It is a tacit admission that some things are missed. Although I feel at home here, there are times when I feel very far away. Today has been one of those days.

30 January 1989   Toto's original owner has suddenly sur-faced. He is a senior from another school who grew up in Korea and is referred to as the "Korean." The "Korean" is a rowdy that nobody likes. There was an altercation when he tried to take the dog away from M—'s dorm. Fortunately, it was hushed up. Later, J— and the "Korean" met behind the gym. The "Korean" did not really want the dog, and let J— keep him for ¥20. It was one-third of J—'s allowance but he gave it to the "Korean."

"Now Toto is really mine." I could hear the happiness in his voice, as we walked along the darkened running track, the hard, frozen earth crunching under foot. The little dog bounded along ahead, growling at unfamiliar shapes that loomed up before him.

31 January 1989   J—appeared on the doorstep after supper. He brushed past me into the apartment and headed straight for the liquor cabinet. "I want to drink something," he said pouring the brandy. "Shall I 'hit you'?" He poured without waiting for an answer. His hand quivered as he handed me the glass. He tried to smile but his face crumpled.

"They took Toto away," he finally choked out.

Security makes surprise inspections of dormitories while students are in class. They search personal belongings for heaven knows what. J— was called on the carpet for having a copy of *Lady Chatterley's Lover*. A— was seriously repri-manded for having a packet of condoms in his suitcase, and made to write a self-criticism. This time it was a puppy.

I can imagine the scene. J— walking into the room after class to find five black-garbed security guards holding his dog. They were going to take him away at once. But J— begged, and the other young men in the room who ap-peared on the scene offered cigarettes and tea. Finally the security guards agreed to let them feed the puppy one last time.

"We gave him a good lunch," J— said, dashing away a tear, "and then they took him away . . ."

I did not have the heart to ask where they took the dog. It does not matter. Some things are better left unknown.

31 January 1989

DEAR NICKY,

I am glad you are thinking of coming to teach here for a while. It will certainly broaden your horizons, and try your patience. It will make you draw on all your reserves of ingenuity, and every trick in the bag to get the job done according to your conscience. Or you can do a little song and dance number and muddle through, as most FEs do. But that is not your style. It might look nice on your resume later, but it won't add to your bank account

It was not the money that brought me here though I live very comfortably on my salary. To work in China one must want to be here. Otherwise it is too hard. Life is difficult in subtle ways. Many things that we take for granted are not available. One has to make compromises daily. It is endlessly frustrating. For example, the seniors have computer class but they seldom see a machine. The thinking is that the less the machine is used the less likely it is to break down. The Tourism Department does not own a decent map, globe, or up-to-date atlas. It took a month of badgering before a map was finally procured. It is true I could have gone downtown myself and bought it. But it is the institute's responsibility to provide proper equipment for its courses. A student whose graduation thesis I am supervising cannot borrow books he needs from the library. The reason: students tend to lose books. I had to borrow the books so he can write his tome. Things like that one either learns to laugh off, or one goes mad.

Universities either house their FEs in the Friendly Hotel or FE buildings on campus. The facilities are pretty standard "theoretically." Some are not so hot. The one at the institute next door does not have central heating. However, there is a crude shower and squat toilet. So it is necessary to ask many questions before coming to terms.

I really cannot complain about the hours. I have eight

classroom hours a week. That gives me time to travel and to write. No matter what you are hired to teach, they will find ways to squeeze English in on a would-you-help-us-out basis. Take everything with a grain of salt. Things change with the prevailing winds, and God knows where they're coming from these days.

There is a certain amount of xenophobia. I really cannot fathom what the Chinese want from foreigners. Aside from the almighty dollar, I don't think they know. They bring us in and try to make us ape their ways while holding us at arm's length. I have a few faculty friends. Friendship with the Chinese faculty is very strenuous and one-sided. They only call on you if they want something. So I leave it entirely to their initiative. I wish they would disappoint me once in a while. But no such luck so far.

31 January 1989   Today was clear but very cold. The trees and even the thistles outside my window have turned into marvelous creations of ice and glitter in the moonlight.

In the afternoon, muffled to the eyebrows, J— and I went to Bei Hai Park to see the ice sculptures. Every winter sculptors from all over the country come here to create dragons and phoenixes, Buddhas and mythological characters, and lanterns of every conceivable shape and size—out of blocks of ice. The lanterns were lit by neon bulbs embedded in the ice. The light refracted into hundreds of flickering rainbows was magical.

The lake was frozen and for a few cents one can rent skates. A ghetto-blaster blared forth waltzes and tangos and couples glided across the ice with great aplomb. The great white bell-shaped dagoba atop the hill gleamed in the sun. It was a beautiful afternoon. Alas, my camera froze. It was only afterwards, sitting in a smokey hole-in-the wall restaurant with a hot pot between us that I realized how cold my feet were. My toes are still ten icicles but the Scotch is beginning to work. No. I'm not soaking my feet in it. Heaven forbid!

5

▶

1 February 1989   "I thought you might be lonely so I
came to visit," Willie smiled, showing a row of ragged teeth.

Indeed, I was glad of some company. I made coffee and
heated up some Danishes for us. Willie wanted to use the
telephone. "This is a good time to talk to people about jobs,"
he said. "It's Spring Festival and they're in a receptive
mood." He winked impishly. He was on the phone for an
hour, cajoling, flattering, telling jokes, being deadly serious. It was an interesting performance to watch and listen
to. When he was done he had five interviews lined up.

"What about your assigned job?" I asked. "Don't you
have to go home?"

Willie made a face. "Home!" he spat the word out as if it
were something dirty.

Willie comes from a primitive farm in the neighboring
province. His grandfather had some small holdings, and
had a rudimentary education. His father and brothers are
barely literate. They live in one house and sleep on a common kang (a sleeping platform of bricks heated by a fire
underneath). On his brother's wedding night, the bridal
pair were separated from the rest of the family by a pair of
sheets hung on either side of them.

"And my father yelled instructions to my brother," Willie
recalled ruefully.

In the winter nobody bathed because there is no hot
water, and clothes and bedding get infested with lice.

"If you came to visit, my father would probably sell

tickets. Nobody has ever seen a foreigner in our village—except me." I refused to believe that, but I suppose there is a grain of truth in what he says. Willie is not anxious to go home, so he is frantically making connections that might help him get a foothold in Beijing.

His real errand this afternoon was to ask me to take him to the Friendship Store. Chinese students are not allowed in, unless accompanied by a foreigner. This sort of thing must create resentment.

Willie wanted to buy Mao Tai (¥186 a bottle, more than the average monthly wage) and foreign cigarettes. We went to the Friendship Store, and I stood back and watched Willie haggle. The lad has a fast tongue and a knack of looking ingenuous even while he's rooking you. He had the sales girl so flustered she sold him the goods for RMB, when she should have charged FEC. Afterwards, I was anxious to leave the store before the girl realized what she had done. But Willie was taking his time, looking at everything. I visualized some security guard pounding after us, demanding FEC.

Willie probably read my mind. "Actually I have FEC. But I prefer to use RMB." I was amazed at the amount of money he had.

Willie said it was a loan. There is an old teacher in his county school who never married and has no family, who hoarded money all his life. Willie was his favorite student. The old man had given him the money and the names of certain people he knew who could help Willie get a job and residence permit in Beijing. When that happens, the old man will come to Beijing and live with Willie for the rest of his life.

I was appalled by the story. The price of the loan seemed outrageous to me, but quite acceptable to Willie. That's the way life is.

Willie has a child bride at home. His parents acquired the girl for him when they were both children. They grew up together, and they are to be married as soon as he graduates. Willie has nothing against the girl, except he does not want to marry her. "What will happen to the girl if you don't go back to your village?" Willie had not considered that at all. He is totally absorbed in himself, and for that reason he will probably go far.

6 February 1989   It's Chinese New Year's Eve and for the second day my apartment was without heat. It was as cold inside as it was out. I was told there was a problem with the boiler. However, there was hot water, and the lobby where the foos lounge about watching TV all day was toasty warm. Something did not jibe.

I went into town because it was impossible to work in the apartment where I could see my own breath. At supper time when I came back to a still frigid apartment, the flash point was reached.

I marched into the lobby and told the foo in charge to stop playing games and turn the heat on. He gaped at me in amazement, then started loudly yammering about the boiler being kaput. But he could see he was getting nowhere with me. They resort to yelling when they're caught in a lie. One way to deal with the Chinese is to keep your cool—ice is the word—and be perfectly correct. That makes them squirm. Then invoke the highest authority of all. "I am going to see the president in his apartment, and lodge a formal complaint," said I.

At six o'clock, Chinese New Year's Eve!

I came back to the apartment for my coat. I had no idea where the president lived. But this charade had to be played to the bitter end. Before I was out the door, the head of Foreign Affairs was on the phone full of apologies. The boiler is being fixed, and would be operative in an hour, he assured me. And the heat came on within the hour.

I have a theory about the "boiler affair." It was probably retaliation because the chief foo's palm was not oiled for the festive occasion. On the other hand we were being perfectly correct, because foos are not "allowed" to accept gifts. A friend who visited a few week ago said that China is confusing and perplexing. It is that even for those of us who have lived and worked here for a while, and have no language barrier to contend with. In spite of all the frustration, these have been two memorable years.

7 February 1989   Campus is almost empty. A few isolated firecrackers explode on the playing fields. There are a few students around, looking forlorn and lost. Chinese New Year is no time to be alone. The ones that are still here either can't afford the trip home, or live too far away.

Y— comes from a village near the western frontier. He does not look like a peasant. He is fair with light brown eyes, finely chiseled cheek-bones and a slender nose. He is one of the brightest in the senior class.

A month ago the dean spoke to me about him. Y— had requested me to supervise his graduation thesis through the dean. "He is a good student." The dean thought he had to do a job of selling. Actually, I was delighted. However, the weeks passed and Y— made no mention of it. Finally I had to broach the subject to him.

Y— ducked his head, and scuffed his toe against the cement floor. "I thought you might be too busy. I know you do a lot of work." Only when he spoke did his peasant origins come out. He required a lot of reassurance. We began to work on his thesis. The library would not lend him the books he needed because they were worth more than ¥50 and he might lose them. However, I took them out without any difficulty. We met twice a week. Y—'s topic, "China and Tourism in Asia," was one that was close to my heart. I had talked about this subject in some detail. Y— drew on that but added thoughts of his own and found material to substantiate his case.

He was terribly diffident, always apologizing for taking my time. He would not accept anything more than a cup of hot water. He is grindingly poor, but proud, and will not accept more than he can reciprocate. For the same reason, he has no friends. He spoke very little of his background except that it is impossible to go home in the winter as it is a two-day trip hitchhiking from the rail-head over a mountain pass. There are frequent avalanches, and the village is snowbound for weeks at a time. The family lives in a cave house cut into the side of a clay cliff, and fronted by a wooden facade with rice paper instead of glass in the windows. Cave houses are warm in winter and cool in summer.

This evening Y— brought his completed thesis for me to read. We did not work. Because it is Chinese New Year, Y— accepted a cup of coffee and a Danish. We talked about his home and how they celebrated the festival. He spoke wistfully of the traditional foods his mother prepared. There was never enough, but everyone got a morsel.

He looks bleakly at the future. Soon he will graduate. He has learned two foreign languages: English and Japanese. He has learned about tourism; he has glimpsed the world beyond his village. But his horizons will contract again. There is no tourism in the region he comes from. Nor is there any potential. He will rusticate.

"If I'm lucky I will become a teacher. But I don't want that."

"What do you want?" I knew I said the wrong thing, but there was no way to take it back. I could see Y— shrinking into himself.

"It doesn't matter. Born a peasant, always a peasant. . . . This society is like that. I will work and my parents will find me a wife and we will make babies." He sighed. His carefully articulated Mandarin had slipped imperceptibly into his western frontier dialect which I had to concentrate to understand. "We all sleep on the same kang. I've watched my parents doing it, and never could figure out what the fuss is all about. Later on they'll watch me," he continued. "I was born in a haystack. That's where my children will be born too."

Life is mechanical, unleavened by love or tenderness. He might have been talking about mating a stud bull in his dull, flat voice. Under the complacency there was deep anger and despair. He had to struggled to get to university. He kept taking the entrance exams until he had overcome all the social, economic, and political obstacles. That is why he is a few years older than the others. He made no friends but acquired the habit of thinking. Now he must unlearn that habit, for thinking would only bring him misery.

He rose to leave. He gripped my hand in both his, and once more apologized for taking my time. I assured him it had been a pleasure working with him, and invited him to visit as often as he liked. He said he would, but he will not be back.

20 February 1989   We live in interesting but troubled times. The reforms are chugging along, dragging in their wake a raft of troubles. Inflation is rampant and there is little faith in the national currency. Everybody scrambles after FEC or dollars. Beggars are quite common these days, especially near the Friendship Store where foreigners go. There is a pitiful old man with a bandaged foot who lies in the middle of the pavement meowing like a sick cat. One morning I went to town early and saw him walking quite normally. Under his voluminous rags he carried a briefcase into which he stuffed wads of money which other beggars on the block handed him as he passed. It was like a scene out of *Oliver Twist*.

Corruption is everywhere. It is almost impossible to get anything done without oiling somebody's palm.

In the midst of change China remains unchanged, and, it seems, unchangeable.

The daily papers are full of anti-corruption reports. Gluttony, in the shape of huge banquets, is a cardinal sin that takes many Hail Marys and Our Fathers to erase. But while the sinners are beating their breasts and crying, "mea culpa, mea culpa, mea MAXIMA culpa," the Mao Tai keeps flowing.

There was a protest on campus two weeks ago. A young teacher (equivalent to lecturer) wrote a big poster and stuck it to the bulletin board in front of the administration building. In it he demanded to know what happened to funds that government had given the institute to improve the living quarters for young teachers. It was intimated that the funds are missing, and that the people who were handling it have also vanished from the campus. Meanwhile, a new faculty apartment building stands vacant due to bureaucratic wrangling as to who should be assigned new quarters. The institute was hosting a very prestigious national seminar of travel managers at the time, and the president was wearing a very long and red face. In the end, the young teacher had his knuckles rapped, and the incident was treated as a storm in a teapot. A rather bad joke after cocktails.

22 February 1989

DEAR GREGORY,

It is the last week of spring break. For the first week or so I was too tired to move. Most of the FEs took off as soon as classes were over, leaving me and a few of the Japanese, who smile and bow, but the lack of a common language makes conversation impossible. It was just as well. I needed time for myself.

Marc, an American FE from New York, wanted me to go with him to Hong Kong, but I declined. So he went off on his own, after exacting a promise that I would take time off writing and go to the south with him. I agreed. Marc is either exuberantly happy or chewing the furniture. We are as unalike as two people can be, but we are both fond of Vivaldi, literature, good education, pasta, whiskey, and doughnuts. There is some common ground.

It was good to get out of Beijing for a while. We took the train to Shanghai then onto Suzhou and Hangzhou and back. It was interesting to watch the landscape change from the dry yellow earth of the north to fields of tender green south of the Yangtze River. People speak a softer, more lilting language. They move more languorously as if their joints were loose. The cuisine is more refined. The shops have a better selection of goods. There are cafes on nearly every street corner, though some will not serve foreigners.

In Hangzhou, my student J— met us and took us sight-seeing. I have read poems about the West Lake since I was knee high. Finally, I was there and it poured with rain! Poets claim West Lake is magical in the rain and they are right. The hills and pavilions, the willows and the pagodas rise like mirages out of the rain. By the end of the day I was swimming in my shoes and the interminable cough that I finally shook came back. But it was worth it.

In the evening J— took us home for dinner to meet his parents. I recognized the apartment building from his descriptions in "Phantoms." In that story he had drawn an accurate if unflattering portrait of his taciturn father. Actually, he is a pleasant man, who is probably more comfortable with mathematical equations than conversation. J—'s stepmother is a tiny woman with a cheery smile. Their southern dialect was a little hard to follow but I managed. J—'s stepmother, who is a physician, prepared the meal, and ran back and forth between kitchen and table. There were mountains of food and much toasting with white lightning. It was very jolly. Even J—'s father loosened up and enjoyed himself.

The family lives in a five-room apartment. After the meal we sat in a book-lined study and watched TV. I was dying to look at the books but was too shy to ask. It was a very pleasant evening.

Later, back in the hotel, Marc mentioned the change in J—. "It's to your credit," he insisted, "and I'm sure Ma and Pa think so too." I shrugged it off. J— is brilliant. All he needed was a bit of encouragement.

27 February 1989   M— sat curled in the sofa surrounded by little heaps of stamps. She has changed in the few weeks that she was home for the spring break. She has the classical almond-shaped face. The horn-rimmed glasses have been replaced by contact lenses. Her eyes are large, black, and lustrous. She has a tiny rosebud of a mouth. Her hair, which used to be pulled back and tied in a knot at the back of her head, had been cut shoulder length and allowed to fall free, framing her face. She was knitting a new scarf in charcoal grey. For the moment the knitting was forgotten, as she sorted the box of stamps I had saved and cadged from the other FEs.

M— has been a part of the group since the travel managers conference. She is bright and ambitious, with a mind of her own. At length, she had all the stamps she wanted, and returned the rest to their box.

"He will be so pleased, teacher," she said in a breathy little voice that can be clear and sharp as steel, as it was when she interpreted at the conference.

Then abruptly, "Teacher, is it all right for a girl of twenty to marry a man of thirty-five?" This is one of the tamer questions I've been confronted with. Nevertheless, it took me by surprise.

M— met Him at the conference, and fell in love. She wants to marry him. "My parents say he's too old, and there's bound to be something wrong with him if he's still a bachelor at thirty-five." She was close to tears.

M— is oldest of three daughters, and doted upon particularly by Mama. Mama, however, sounds like a dragon. "When I'm home she locks me in my room at nine o'clock every night. I can't even go to a movie. When I'm at school, she phones long-distance every night at seven to check on me. She loves me!" The girl threw her hands up in exasperation. "He wants to travel south to meet my parents but Mama won't receive him."

I suggested the man should go anyway. Surely the parents would not turn him away from their doorstep.

28 February 1989

Dear Kurt & Crystal,

President Bush's state visit was highlighted by a ride up and down Changan Street during which Mr. B. screeched "*Ni hao, ni hao*"at the startled populace through a megaphone. Then there was a lugubrious interview on CCTV in which a great many words were used to say very little. Said Mr. B., "You have problems—we have problems—let's put our problems together," or something to that effect.

Problems in Paradise? Nah. Impossible!

The weather forecast calls for unsettled conditions. Now there's a catchy phrase for you.

Today's *China Daily* quotes Zhao Zhiyang's response to Mr. Bush. Said he, "There are those who think the reform has developed on the wrong track and should be reversed. There are others who regard the difficulties as political in nature and urge solutions based on Western models. The first group will get no support from the people, whereas the other group, a handful of people with the intention of provoking social unrest, completely ignores the particular circumstances in China, and is therefore not feasible. If the latter view prevailed, the reform would encounter obstacles which would cause setbacks and have serious consequences." Unquote.

An interesting tidbit of the Bush visit. The president gave a banquet to which the Chinese astrophysicist Fang Lizhi and his wife were invited. However, they were barred from the hall by security guards. The story was carried by the *Hong Kong Standard*, but ignored by *China Daily*. Curious. Ironically, a few weeks ago, a bulletin entitled "An Urgent Message" appeared on a campus bulletin board, whose main thrust was the need for stringent measures to control population growth. But it veered off on a tangent and concluded that even if the population was kept down, "even if we did not become dominated by Western ideas; were not attacked or drawn into someone else's war; do not fall victim to natural catastrophes, we would still be a Third World country by 2040, if the reforms continue at the present rate." Frightening? Perhaps.

Indeed, the times are a-changing. Everybody is scrambling after the almighty dollar (or FEC). Students are out hustling when they don't come to class. One Chinese faculty member gave me a half-hour harangue at a recent soirée whining how Chinese youth is being lured off the straight and narrow by awful Western materialism. Yet, all the while, he knows that I know he's been too ill to teach, but not too ill to be raking in FEC moonlighting at a joint venture hotel. Everybody wants FEC these days.

Last week, the *China Daily* announced next year Paradise will no longer import foreign booze and cigarettes. Yesterday, I bagged the last bottle of Glenleven at the Friendly Store for an unconscionable price. There were no American cigarettes, coffee, or jam. The shelves were all but bare. The money-changing boys under the Jianguomen overpass carry knives. Everybody is edgy.

I spent half of my spring vacation traveling to Shanghai, Suzhou, and Hangzhou, then went north to Harbin for the tail end of the Ice LanternFestival. Traveling in Paradise has always been an obstacle course to me, but I am pleased to report the soft sleepers were actually quite enjoyable. Locals and foreigners were kept firmly apart. There have been a number of train accidents lately. Farmers in remote areas were stealing and selling the tracks. Thus, every lurch of the train sent my pulse racing. But, as you see, I am back in one piece. Shanghai had frequent blackouts because there was a shortage of coal to generate electricity. Someone had been quietly shoveling it out the back door. The money changers look and act like Sicilian mafiosi. The stores are jammed with goods not seen in Beijing. The bookstalls feature Paradise's answer to *Playboy*. In Shanghai there is a bar or cafe on practically every corner. But most of the bars and cafes outside of the tourist hotels will not serve foreigners. Said one evening-dressed maitre d', "We'll lose our license if we let you in."

In Beijing there is even a ring that counterfeits bus tickets. The public security has been on TV urging bus-users to examine their tickets. Just how the scam works is more than this feeble brain can handle.

Ah, these blessed halls of ivy! How they protect us from the growing madness outside!

Not entirely. The ruckus with the African students in Nanjing was only the tip of the iceberg called "Xenophobia." It began when a Chinese girl was refused admission to a Christmas party given by African students on the Nanjing

University campus. There was an exchange of words between an African student and the security guard, which escalated to a bit of push and shove. Then someone hit a well-loved professor who tried to intervene, and all hell broke loose. There have been similar incidents in other cities involving Africans. The Chinese assure me there is no racial prejudice here. They just don't prefer certain types. Thus far the blacks have taken the brunt of it, but I wonder for how long.

There are many Christians (Southern Baptists and Mormons) who are proselytizing quite openly. One creature who taught English here last year included the Ten Commandments in his final exam paper. This sort of thing does not win friends and influence people. This year's 4th of May theme once more extols the virtues of nationalism and self-reliance, which sounds isolationist and almost blatantly xenophobic. Your commentator does not know what to make of it. Wait and see.

26 March 1989 (Easter)   This morning I went to mass at the church I used to attend as a child. Last year it was still closed. Since then it has been restored and now it is functioning. The church is in the old legation quarter, where the foreign missions and embassies used to be. The streets are lined with fine old trees, and interspersed with small parks. What used to be the bridle-path is now a pleasant promenade. Empty stone pedestals remain where statues once stood. I remember Frau Henschel, the grotesque fat wife of the German Ambassador who lived several houses down the road from us, tearing down the bridle-path on her rickety steed, shrieking "Ho-yo-ho! Ho-yo-ho!" She fancied herself an opera singer! Some of the big old houses are shuttered now while others brim with life. All are crumbling. There is a sad, faded elegance about the area, like the lingering scent of perfume when the wearer has left the room. I stopped in front of an old house built in the German style where we lived while my father was building his.

Traces of yellow paint and white trim were still visible under decades of grime. However, the house my father built no longer stands.

For a while I was in another age, when life was gracious. I walked the street as a child again, accompanied by Rex, the Great Dane that was my constant companion. The dog used to wait outside the vestry door, while inside I struggled into my choir robes and Father Vonnegut gave the final directions for the mass. The church was always half empty when I was small. It also seemed a lot larger then, perhaps because of our relative sizes. Sometimes I wondered whether our singing could be heard at all in that vastness. Father V. always said God heard. Now the church is packed to the gunwales, and spilling into the churchyard.

I was late, dawdling down Memory Lane, and could not get in. I stood on the steps outside. Above the hubbub, I could hear the organ, and the choir singing a chorus from *Messiah* in Chinese. The mass was over quickly. As the people streamed out, I squeezed in. I sat in the shadow of a great pillar, breathing in the smell left by close-packed bodies in winter clothes, guttering candles, and incense, and listening for the clatter of childish footsteps down the choir stairs, and the welcoming bark of the dog outside that belong to another time. I felt immensely peaceful and content. It is moments like these that make me feel I could stay forever. But it is illusion. One can never really go home again.

My life is simple. I teach, I study, I write. I seem to be the busiest FE in the building. This ship of fools is full of eccentrics, malcontents, and other oddities. I move among them trying not to become involved with any clique. In fact, what spare time I have is often spent in the company of students. I fear I am becoming something of a Mr. Chips—with Chinese characteristics. There is a small circle that has grown around me. Many are from the university I taught at last year. These young men and women ride their bicycles two hours each way to visit, sometimes in bitter cold. My apartment becomes quite animated at such times.

There will usually be a group cooking a meal in the

kitchen; another glued to the TV watching some ancient American film dubbed in Chinese (excruciating Shirley Temple epics on Sunday afternoons that Chinese viewers love); and an ongoing game of Go, a very ancient form of chess that I am slowly learning. Willie, one of the lads who is teaching me, complains I am driving him to distraction with my ineptness. I tell him now he knows how I feel when I read his papers.

These young people are far more interesting than my peers. They are poised on the brink of life, in an age of change; hopeful of the future, but fearful too. The rumblings of discontent are muffled by layers of censorship and deceit. But it is there. Now and then it breaks to the surface: the trouble with the blacks in Nanjing; the riots in Tibet; the rampant corruption, the confused economy, the reforms that seem to start and stop and go nowhere. These young people are closer to it all than any of us. Particularly foreigners who must forever be on the periphery of life in China. I am very fortunate to have their friendship.

24 March 1989   The opera season opened with *Tosca* presented by the PLA (People's Liberation Army) Opera Company. This must surely be the world's most unusual army. Aside from opera, it also has a very good ballet, theatre, art and literature departments. For instance, Mo Yen, the author of the acclaimed *Red Sorghum*, is a soldier in the army's literary department. The opera company has its own theatre, which is massive, and quite beautiful in the ponderous Russian style. Although it needs lightness to soften the austere straight lines and grey unadorned walls, acoustically it is superb.

My companions for the evening were "Their Eminences," Dick and Maisy; the Russian student, Dmitri, and Greta, the eccentric Belgian, who are having an affair. I do not belong in this circle. I got involved with this lot strictly by chance. Dick saw the ad in *China Daily* and offered to get the tickets. Dick and Maisy really aren't that bad, if one ignores the airs and graces of Duluth high society. That I can manage quite well, thank you.

The opera house is on the opposite end of the city. Two long bus rides and a fairly long walk in a blustery gale later, we were finally in our seats in the stalls. We left campus at 4:30, stopped for a quick meal, and here we were just in time for a 7:30 curtain. Maisy was sounding off about a night at the Met. I listened with half a mind. My mind switches off when she starts whining through her nose. The images that flashed through my head were like stills from old movies. Maisy with her "naturally curly hair" as Garbo clutching a bunch of camelias and Dick dancing attendance, fidgeting with his fly. There was a kifufle over seating between Greta and Dmitri. The Russian huffed off and found a seat some-where else. Greta pouted. I waited for the house lights to go down, wondering when the Marx Brothers would show up.

Tosca was sung in Chinese. I am again amazed how well Chinese adapts itself to Italian music. One of the joys of opera in China is that the performers are usually quite young and look their parts as well as sing them. Mario had the open-throated sound of the young Placido Domingo, but some annoyingly effete posturing. Tosca was too sweet-faced but her warm dark soprano worked well in a role that often becomes screechy. Scarpia was very tall, and pale. Almost like Christopher Lee in *Dracula*. Here was an actor with presence. He dominated the stage even in moments when he had little or nothing to do, as during Tosca's "Vissi d'arte." He stood gazing out the window up-stage. Al-though Tosca was singing on her knees, and finally flings herself face down on the floor for the finale, I was watching Scarpia. He conveyed such a feeling of violence barely held in check that the murder, when it happens, fairly explodes, losing none of its impact through familiarity. The director was probably influenced by Zefferelli's staging for Maria Callas. There was a great deal of movement, but never for its own sake. Elsewhere these singing actors would be stars. Here their names don't even appear on the billboard! The rest of the season will be *Turandot, Carmen, Madame Butter-fly,* and a new Chinese opera.

Tonight I am going to the National Theatre's *Galileo* by Brecht. It will also be in Chinese.

9 April 1989

DEAR SUSAN,

A group of us went up the Great Wall at Mutienyu yesterday. Though not as high as the more well-traveled section at Badaling, Mutienyu is more rugged. I went off on my own to explore a section of the wall that had not been restored.

Following the ruins up a steep incline I climbed to the top of a ridge where there were the remnants of a fort. It was the first warm spring day. Trees and hillsides were beginning to show hints of green. It was sunny and the air was clear. The whole valley was spread out below. Terraced farms and cave-houses dotted the hillsides. The fields were all ploughed but still waiting for the seeds to sprout. In a few weeks they will be green. But now the earth is still bare. Overhead, a few hawks circled lazily. I ate my picnic, rested awhile, then walked up a bit further. You cannot imagine the relief of having no one else around. That is a luxury in China.

I stayed longer than I should, and then had to hurry down and pulled a muscle at the back of my right knee. Today I'm hobbling with a great ugly bandage on my leg. But it really looks worse than it feels.

9 April 1989

MY DEAR RUSS & WENDY,

Thank you for the delightful birthday card which finally got here.

There have been a few unpleasantries in the building of late and we are being punished by having the mail delayed. The truth is some of the "inmates" are on the verge of cracking up. China is not a place to be if one is unstable. Marc, my upstairs neighbor, precipitated this last confrontation. Marc hides a sackful of insecurities behind his bluster and bravado, and what he calls "Mediterranean temperament." One of his horrors is aging. He cooked dinner for me on my birthday. It was a pleasant evening until the wine took effect. Marc is a nasty drunk, and the jokes became less than funny as the evening progressed. The next day he had a hangover and was apologetic. "Look, Doc," (he calls me Doctor for some reason), "I'll be forty in a few weeks. You have to get me through it!" His eyes bulged in a peculiar demented way that troubled me. I tried to make light of it. But Marc was really panicked. He rambled on incoherently about his hair falling out, his body losing definition, his girl friend, his inability to establish meaningful friendships, this cold, calculating society we live in. . . . All this was leading up to a confession of his lust for a nineteen-year-old girl, newly arrived from Germany. The seduction of Helena would reaffirm his manhood, he insisted.

I am not a prude but Marc's stock slipped considerably. Helena has the sweet innocence of a Renaissance madonna. Overnight, Marc had turned into a drooling Humbert Humbert sniffing at her heels. But I needn't have been concerned about Helena. She was wily and led Marc a merry chase. She never went anywhere without her sidekick Anna. And Anna, the plainer of the two, played duenna with relish. They soon had Marc dancing on a string between them. Marc is on edge and drinking heavily. The seduction that was to prove he still "has it," has gone terribly awry. He is so anxious to hang on to youth, he has reverted to behaving like a spoiled teenage brat.

The rule of the house is that visitors have to register at the front desk. One evening an American friend from another campus visited Marc, and refused to sign in on the grounds that it interfered with his "human rights." There was an argument. Marc, who takes everything as a personal insult, had a shouting match with Uncle Panda. Uncle P., the crusty old bird who mans the counter at night, tends to be stiff, particularly if he thinks *his* "human rights" are being trampled on. Which is nearly all the time. Marc would have slugged him if he weren't an old man. Instead he put his fist through the hallway window.

Mid-March was bitterly cold. The heat came on from sundown to midnight only. The wind howling through the building did not help. The administration was not in a hurry to replace the pane. By the end of that week, the building was flu city.

There were endless and embarrassing meetings to study the cause of this unhappy incident. More importantly, to discover who was at fault. None of this endeared the perpetrator to the rest of us. Marc eventually ate crow and the glass was replaced.

The devils tend to tar everyone with the same brush. The mail was deliberately withheld as a punishment.

In the old days the Emperor slaughtered a few hundred to make a point. This was less vicious but in the same spirit. This comedy of errors also says something about the calibre of FEs. Some are just not suitable for life in this society.

9 April 1989   I went into town today on a silly errand— to the foreign language book store, not to buy but to look. My first translation project was displayed in the section marked "New Books." I have waited a long time for this moment: to stand in a bookstore, in front of rows and rows of new books that was my work. As so often happens in China, there were glitches. The cover design is conservative and insipid. Also the publisher included several stories by the same author that had been previously published and translated by other people. Still, it was a good feeling.

Afterwards I took myself to the top of the CITIC tower and treated myself to an absolutely disgusting buffet lunch. Smoked salmon, salads, cold cuts, hot dishes, and Sacher Torte. Decadence is delightful!

10 April 1989   J. L. and his wife are really the nicest people I know. They are both aging very noticeably. Particularly Mrs. J. L, who is getting very senile. But she is always pleased to see me, and speaks to me in English though the conversation wanders. They are trying to get their daughter transferred from Tianjin to look after them, which is a major hassle. Everyone has a residential registration, and you live wherever your registration happens to be. Without it you are a non-person, deprived of ration tickets, medical care, etc., etc. During the Cultural Revolution J. L. was sent to the country, and Mrs. was sent to Tianjin. When it was over, J. L. was brought back here but not his wife. Legally, she is supposed to be in Tianjin. However, she has been an "illegal" resident of Beijing for the last 10 years. J. L.'s petition to have their daughter moved here was refused on the grounds that there was no need for the move since Mrs. J. L. was already a resident of Tianjin, and her daughter was also living in that city. The only solution is to have Mrs. J. L.'s registration changed. That is baying at the moon. However, there are ways of getting round these obstacles, if the right palms are oiled.

22 April 1989

My Dear —,

Unfamiliar sounds wake me. I lay in the dark, conscious that something had wakened me but not knowing what. Then I heard the rain; the second time in almost a year, and the sound made me homesick. Suddenly I felt very far away.

I am glad you kept my runners. There was no deep significance except that they would be there when we go to the beach again. I miss the ocean. Spring is upon us and the campus is quite lovely. But the landscape is flat. The mountains and the ocean are far away.

Part Two

▶

Distant Thunder

1

▶

10 April 1989   The winter is over. But there is a stiff wind, and the dust eddies whirl down the streets whistling and squealing. The trees are a smudge of such tender green that one is not sure it is there. In a few days there will be leaves. But now there is just a blush of green, a harbinger of spring. Dinner at N—'s. We are good companions. There is a good deal of gentle joshing when either one or the other becomes too serious. I sometimes wonder about N—'s life. It is not easy being a widow. But she is not a typical Chinese woman. She is an intellectual with a mind of her own and a fierce independence. Veronica once described her as "intimidating." But I have never found her that way. It was a cozy meal. N—, her granddaughter S—, who will be going to university in September, and I. The TV was tuned to CCTV's evening news. It was the usual pap. Production quotas met; criminals apprehended looking battered; and the "Fossil Club" attending the latest session of the Central Committee of the Chinese Communist Party. It is amazing how old the delegates are. There was scarcely a face under 60 in the hall.

"Have you heard of Hu Yaobang?" asked N— as the news ended. I had. He was the ousted predecessor of Zhao Ziyang, the Party chief. "Hu Yaobang is attending the congress this year," she went on. "He usually calls in sick." I was amazed that he was even allowed to attend. A Western politician in disgrace would have vanished to his farm to write his memoirs.

Later we were joined by two other professors. H—, a square-faced fellow with an ingratiating smile, teaches English. He also paints landscapes and carried an album of photographs of his work. He has been to the Pacific Northwest, which explains the obviously North American scenery he paints from memory. D— is older, and taught English until he retired last year. A portly man with a stoop, he paced nervously up and down, hands folded behind his back, peering at the rest of us like an old owl, his eyes enlarged by thick spectacles. He has been compiling yet another English-Chinese dictionary, and recounting the latest skirmish with his editor. "Well, it's all here," he said, triumphantly patting the bulky manuscript in his shoulder bag. "And they're not getting their sticky fingers on it, until . . ."

Once again the conversation turned to Hu Yaobang. I was content to sip tea and listen.

Hu Yaobang was an unusual man. Born in 1915 in Liuyang County, Hunan Province, he took part in the communist-led peasant revolt when he was in his teens, and later joined the Long March. After the founding of the People's Republic in 1949 he became the first secretary of the Central Committee of the Chinese Communist Youth League. He suffered during the '60s, but he survived and rose to China's highest position, general secretary of the Communist party in the early '80s. He did much to restore order after the Cultural Revolution and redress some of the injustices committed during those ten years of turmoil from 1966 to 1976.

A liberal who recognized the country's dire need to improve education, Hu's greatest contribution was championing the cause of intellectuals. In 1978 at the first scientific congress held in Beijing in a decade, he publicly stated the country's need to grasp the world's newest advances in science and technology. It was the beginning of the thaw that restored many intellectuals, including N—, to the jobs they had before the Cultural Revolution.

He was hounded out of office in 1987 for his liberal views. Politicians in disgrace vanish from public view. Since then he has seldom been mentioned.

Although he retained his membership in the Politburo of

the Central Committee, Hu has not attended meetings since his ouster. There was much speculation as to what brought him back. The main item of business of the latest session was the chaotic economy. Chinese do not address problems as we do. They are less interested in finding remedies when things go wrong than a scapegoat to blame it on. One speculation was that Hu was about to be used as scapegoat. Another conjecture was that he was about to be reinstated, as Zhao Ziyang was rapidly losing credibility.

All three intellectuals in the room benefitted from Hu's policies. Yet each saw the man in a different light. The consensus was that Hu Yaobang is a decent, reasonably intelligent man. He had good ideas but he did not have the backing to implement them. Reform in education is still empty talk. Teachers grumble about salaries that are this side of the poverty line, and the lack of housing. Teaching material was either unavailable or out of date. Opportunities for further education abroad were few and dogged by nepotism. Corruption is rife in the halls of ivy. *China Daily* and CCTV report what they are told. Literature, art, and music ape Western styles. H— hastily pointed out that not all painters followed Western conventions. There is a distinctly Chinese characteristic to his work which he proceeded to explain using the pictures in his album. H— had deftly steered the conversation to his art. While N— and I listened, D— continued his pacing.

"I hear Hu Yaobang is going to read a paper," D— said suddenly.

D— cited impeccable sources showing off his impressive connections. But Hu Yaobang as a subject for conversation was worn out. Shortly afterwards the party broke up .

12 April 1989   The original plan was having an early dinner at N—'s and going to a new film. But the film had been taken off. N—, S— and I had supper and watched TV instead. N— commented that there was no mention of Hu Yaobang. Should there have been, I asked. According to a (reliable) friend of N—'s, Hu had tried to present a paper several times during the week. But he was blocked at each turn. On the last occasion, which was several days ago, there was an angry exchange between him and Premier Li Peng. Hu is said to have collapsed after the session and was rushed to hospital.

The Snows of Kilamanjaro came on dubbed with reedy Chinese voices. The last five minutes were lopped off. Susan Hayward comes out of the tent. She sees the plane approaching. The dying Gregory Peck wakes and sees it too. The plane bumps onto the ground. Susan Hayward hugs Gregory Peck. He is saved. They smile into the camera. Fade out. A happy ending. Why not?

15 April 1989   I spent the day writing, and only emerged from my apartment at supper time. I had not eaten all day and was ready for a double serving of noodles with meat sauce. As I went down the corridor Mr. Ito was hurrying towards me, the sleeves and skirt of his kimono flapping like great wings. Mr. Ito, who never hurries, was scurrying along as if ten devils were after him. I stepped aside to let him pass. As he did he whispered out of the corner of his mouth, "Hu Yaobang . . . dead . . . "   Before I could respond he turned up one of the stairwells and vanished.

There was hardly a soul in the dining hall. I shoveled down two plates of noodles, knowing I would pay for my gluttony within the hour. All the while, Mr. Ito's cryptic words knocked about in my brain. Mr. Ito was obviously perplexed by the news. If it had been Deng Xiaoping there might be cause for excitement. But this was the death of a disgraced politician. Why would that upset the inscrutable Mr. Ito?

There was no mention of Hu Yaobang in the news tonight. Perhaps Mr. Ito, or whoever he heard it from, was wrong.

27 April 1989

Dear Mark & Nick,

I don't know how much of these troubled times has been reported by your press. It could become serious.

As I write this in the safety and quiet of my apartment, many of my students are on Tiananmen Square. This is the fifth day of demonstrations.

This afternoon I went into town to hear Montserrat Caballe in recital, not knowing there was a curfew. The center of the city was ringed with troops and sealed tight as a drum. The buses stopped several kilometers east of the Square. I got off and walked. The sidewalks were jammed. The roadway was filled with stalled cars which had overheated, and bicycles tangled wheels with one another. Police whistles shrilled everywhere. I got as far as the railway station and realized that it was impossible to get to the Concert Hall which was further west. I abandoned the idea of the concert, but getting back was a problem too.

It was rush hour, and an increasing crowd milled around the number 9 bus stop. I met a couple of girls from the senior class on their way to the Square. M— and C— were bewildered and tired.

"Come with us, teacher," said M—. "Everybody will be there." "It's fun," chimed her friend C—. "Fun?" I exclaimed, suddenly angry. The city was half paralyzed, and I was unable to hear Caballe after moving heaven and earth for a ticket. And it was "fun!" "You think we're silly," said M—, the sober one of the two. I shrugged. What is it to me? I am a foreigner, who will go home one day and all this will be just another memory.

"You must come," insisted M—. "You've said yourself in class that we must be aware of the world around us. But you're shutting us out."

The reproach struck home. I tried to explain I was not shutting anything out. I was not getting involved. There is a difference. I tried to persuade them that what they thought of as fun is seen as something quite the opposite by the authorities. I pointed out they could get into serious trouble and begged them to come back with me. But they would not.

"We walked here from campus and we're not going back," said C—. The childish gleam in her eye, a moment ago, vanished. Suddenly there was a look of such grim purpose that I swallowed whatever else I had to say.

"Very well," I said. "But don't get into trouble."

They melted into the crowd waving cheerily.

It was hellish getting back. The buses had stopped and the jitneys were jammed to bursting. The crowd got thicker by the minute, and its frustration was turning it ugly. I leaped on the next jitney that slowed down, not even bothering to ask its destination. We inched forward, detoured down back alleys, threaded through tortuous *hutongs** of old dilapidated courtyard houses, and finally emerged on Changan Street near the Friendship Store. I was lucky it was going east.

The first vague hint of trouble on the horizon was at dinner two weeks ago, when N— casually mentioned that Hu Yaobang was ill in hospital. He died on Saturday, 15 April, but the news was not released till the following Monday.

China Daily came out with a black border around its front page, and the banner headline was: "HU MOURNED AS GREAT MAN." A portrait of Hu dominated the page. It was a curious face. The left eye was smaller than the other. The nose was broad and flat. The mouth was delicately shaped, like a woman's. It was not the face of a statesman or even a politician. It was more the face of a shrewd businessman.

The reaction was dramatic. News of the death had leaked to the students of Beijing University during the weekend. Elegiac poems and couplets appeared on bulletin boards almost immediately. The students at People's University and the Academy of Art followed suit. The institute is in the eastern suburbs on the other side of the city and the news did not reach us till Monday morning.

An unusually subdued senior class met that morning. My usual "Good morning, ladies and gentlemen" met with stony silence. Willie was the first to speak up. "Do you

hutongs are lanes or alleyways.

know what happened?" "Yes," I replied. "I'm very sorry." "What do you think of Hu Yaobang?" someone else asked. I felt the hairs on the back of my neck bristle. It was an instinctive warning system that I could be walking into a mine field. "I don't know enough to form an opinion." "But he is dead," said one of the girls, as though that fact alone demanded some comment. "Every man's death diminishes me for I am involved with Mankind." My mind grabbed the words from memory's bag of tricks. Willie's fixed grin disappeared as he grappled the unfamiliar words. . . . M—'s eternal knitting went on without missing a stitch. Nancy scribbled furiously, writing down every word I uttered. Y— stared at me, eyes shining like marbles. Wally gazed out the window nodding with the cadence of the words. A—'s empty seat, gaped like a missing front tooth. C—, a pretty girl, tittered. J—'s lips moved silently forming the words with me. "Therefore, send not to ask: 'For whom the bell tolls.' It tolls for thee . . ." Dust motes danced in the light that shafted through the windows. You could hear a pin drop in the room. Then all at once a great sigh. I opened my notes and began the lecture.

By the next morning the campus had taken on a different appearance. Big posters, and poems scrawled on leaves out of notebooks covered all the bulletin boards. Someone had written, "Yaobang, you went too soon!" across my blackboard. It was an oral class and I did not have to use the blackboard or I would have been in trouble.

The students of Beijing University, the University of Politics and Law, and China Youth Political Institute created huge wreathes which they laid at the foot of the Monument to the People's Heroes in the center of Tiananmen Square. Thousands gathered there. The silent vigil went on day and night. I thought the police would surely put a stop to it. But they did not.

Hu Yaobang, vilified in life, had become a "great statesman, and thinker," an "outstanding leader and a true friend of the people." Zhao Ziyang, speaking before the Central Committee on the urgent need for reform in education, maintained that Hu's farsighted view on the importance of education was an example to follow. His life was reviewed with the reverence reserved for saints.

Where but in China can a disgraced politician become an icon? The question is who was making Hu a symbol and to what ends? Was it the media? *China Daily* and CCTV are both toadies of the state. Why was the state making such a great fuss over a man it had discarded? The other possibility was that it was a spontaneous show of grief by students and intellectuals whom Hu championed. Again there was a troubling false note. First of all, the Chinese are not given to public demonstrations of grief. Secondly, it was too organized. Chinese students are not used to group activities. Left to their own devices, they could not organize a picnic without endless bickering. Someone had to be directing them from the wings. Who?

All Thursday, the twentieth, people streamed into the Square carrying wreaths. The students of the Central Academy of Art created a six-meter-long portrait of Hu Yaobang which was hung on the monument. An honor guard, arms raised above their heads and hands linked, ringed the monument. The photograph on the front page of *China Daily* sent chills up my spine. There was a steely quality in the gleam of the eyes and the set of the mouths of these students that was frightening. Campus was almost emptied. There was a holiday atmosphere. Most of them were going on a lark. Anything was better than the monotonous round of classes. Faculty members whispered together behind closed doors. The dean was smoking again.

That night, several hundred students gathered outside Zhongnanhai, that part of the Forbidden City where the heads of state live, with wreaths and a petition. The petition was in seven parts: some of the demands were disclosure of politicians' earnings and property holdings; separation of the judiciary from the party; putting an end to bureaucratic corruption; better treatment for intellectuals; more funding for education; freedom of the press. They were stopped by guards wielding electric prods and clubs. There was a riot. Stones and bottles were thrown. Some people were injured. One student, a young girl, was killed by a police car. The

official story was that she ran in front of an oncoming bus.
The crowd finally dispersed at dawn. From then on emotions ran high. While the state funeral was being planned
the city was gripped by tension. Friday afternoon (21 April)
I went to the Square. The bus was so packed I thought I
would end up with broken ribs.

Thousands were gathered on the Square. The huge portrait of Hu the students of the Art Academy created gazed
implacably from the monument, the base of which was
banked with wreaths and bouquets. The students linked
hands round the monolith. Every inch of the terrace and the
steps leading up was occupied. But there was hardly a
sound. People stood shoulder to shoulder. When they spoke
at all, it was in whispers. I got onto the steps of the monument and looked back. All I could see were heads spread
across the Square. The air crackled with tension. The faces
turned to the monument were sad, angry, and troubled.
Many were students. Others were intellectuals of one stripe
or another. Some were simple country folk. All were bound
by a common grief. The silence was oppressive and eerie,
but also beautiful in a terrifying way. I saw a very old man
with a long white beard sitting cross-legged on the ground,
holding a wooden staff. By his clothes, I would guess he was
from the country. He sat staring up at the monument,
intense grief written all over his face. I wondered where he
came from, and what he was thinking. I wanted to speak to
him, but in the end did not have the heart to intrude. For it
would have been an intrusion.

I threaded my way across the Square to the Forbidden
City. In the shadow of the vermillion walls were six buses
full of soldiers. It made me tremble. Emotions were running
so high that anything could lead to violence.

Saturday morning (22 April) the Square was cordoned off
for the funeral. Foreigners were strictly forbidden anywhere
near. I watched the proceedings on TV. Changan street was
lined ten deep. They were all there: Deng Xiaoping, who
raised Hu to prominence then destroyed his political career.
Zhao Ziyang, the moderate party chief who succeeded him.
Li Peng, the stone-faced conservative premier. Yang Shang-

kun, Deng's comrade-in-arms. The national anthem and "The Internationale" were played; the eulogies and the crocodile tears were broadcast live. Outside, thousands of students filled the Square. The police had broadcast a warning the night before that the Square had to be cleared, but had taken no steps to do so.

As the funeral cortege moved out of the Great Hall, the students surged forward with hands linked. Silent and orderly, a black tide engulfed the hearse. So it was, all the way westward along Changan Street. What we did not see on TV was the charge of the police wielding clubs and cattle prods. There were many injuries and arrests. The situation turned ugly. This outpouring of grief reminds many of a similar demonstration after the death of Zhou Enlai. It also reminds them of the repression it led to. The intelligensia will be looking over their shoulders again.

Sunday (23 April) was an ominously quiet day. One has the feeling that the fragile quiet may shatter at any moment. There were few students visible and no visitors. Not even J—. I did not leave the apartment until dusk. Although ours is a rather somnolent campus away from the major universities, which are in the western suburbs, posters were everywhere. "Yaobang lives forever". . . "Yaobang, how shall we recall your spirit ". . . "His soul is marching on" echoing the "Battle Hymn of the Republic." Hu in death had become a martyr and a rallying point. The posters denounced the government for its callousness towards the people and its flagrant corruption. The students, as the conscience of the people, demanded to be heard. What was most disturbing was the cry for democracy, freedom of speech, and even revolution. Up to this point the government has shown remarkable tolerance. But my suspicious foreign mind does not see it that way. The government is looking for a scapegoat, and all the talk of democracy and freedom of speech is playing right into their hands. These are foreign ideas that came from opening to the West.

Crowds drifted from one bulletin board to another. I spotted C—'s bald pate in a small group of political leaders from all departments on the periphery of the crowd. There were many strangers. People exchanged glances, not acknowledging each other. They were making mental notes of each other's presence for the future. I moved about as quietly as possible. But it is extremely hard to be inconspicuous. I try to ignore the curious stares. "How much do you understand?" a voice asked beside me.

"Every word," I answered.

"I see."

I turned and looked into the bland face of the president. We exchanged nods, and he moved on. I have no idea how long he had been standing beside me. A young teacher who was copying the posters into a notebook scampered after him. The president is a heavyset man with a stoop. He walked with shoulders hunched and hands folded behind his back. The young teacher was babbling excitedly into his ear. The president nodded, his head moving in rhythm with his footsteps. They disappeared together into the darkened administration building.

Late that night the more militant students of our neighboring college breached the wall that separates our two campuses and went into the boys' dorm. In the early hours I was wakened from a confused and terrifying dream by a drum beating in the quadrangle. My windows face the other direction and all I could see was flickering firelight reflected in the windows of the empty new building on the other side of the garden. A mob was chanting in English, "Foreigners come out! Foreigners come out!" Our students had joined the movement.

"Damned fools!" I swore to myself. "What do they think they'll accomplish!"

Somewhere a window smashed. A girl screamed; then cheers and laughter and more chanting. It dawned on me that they were shouting for the foreign students to join them. By the sound of the hubbub, the foreign students were climbing out of their windows. They are locked in their building just as we are at night. A high-pitched voice shouted directions that echoed round the quadrangle. The shouting continued for a long time.

I lay trembling, in the dark. I remember thinking of that

Monty Python foot in the sky, and saying to myself, "Here it comes." It was almost a palpable weight pressing down on my head. But after the first moments of terror, the cacophony of echoing voices and drums washed over me and whirled me about. I tingled with excitement. If I could have squeezed between the bars across my windows I would have climbed out and joined them. Yet another part of my brain said coldly, "Don't be a fool. You're a foreigner. It's none of your affair. Keep out of it."

Towards daybreak things quieted and I dozed.

Monday (24 April) I went to class bleary-eyed. It was midterm exam. As I crossed the quadrangle to my classroom, someone hailed me from the boys' dorm. I glanced at my watch and walked over to the ground floor window. Every inch of space in the room was taken. The room was so full of cigarette smoke I could barely see some of the faces.

"Did we wake you?" "You did." "Do you know what is happening?" "Tell me." "We're on strike," said T—, grinning like the Cheshire cat. "Don't go to class today." "Your government pays me a lot of money to be here," I said. "I have a job to do."

"But this movement is important," said Z— with more heat than I thought he was capable of. "The people have taken all the abuse they can handle. We have to do something!"

"My job is to teach," I said. "Your job is to learn. So let's get the job done." I glanced at my watch again. "Five minutes." I started to walk away.

"Sir . . ." That word stopped me dead in my tracks. They have been told never to use it on me. It was T— again. I turned and our glances locked. "We won't be there. Only the girls will show up."

"If one person shows up I will be there."

"Will you give the exam. . . ." T—'s voice had lost its edge. The others had quieted.

"Yes. You have five minutes . . ." I wheeled around and walked quickly toward the classroom building. My heart was hammering against my ribs. What if nobody comes? I pushed open the door. To my surprise two-thirds of the seniors were there.

I greeted the class with my usual, "Good morning, ladies and gentlemen." There was no response. They were pale, and haggard from lack of sleep. It doesn't take much to make these ill-fed young people hollow-eyed.

A hand shot up. "Do you know what's going on?" demanded Willie. "Yes." "What is your opinion?" Willie persisted, eyes gleaming. Willie is a fervent Party member. For a moment my mind went blank. I heard myself speaking as from a distance. "I haven't one. If you invited me to your home, and when I arrived you were quarreling with your father, what should I do?" Willie looked at me blankly. Someone muttered unintelligibly at the back of the room. "It's exactly the same situation," I said.

The others started to drift in. T— and Z— and a few of the usual absentees stayed away. I gave the test as though nothing untoward had happened, and promised a separate test for those who did not attend.

During the next hour C—, the political leader, stuck his head through the window of my ground floor classroom. I saw him out of the corner of my eye but chose not to acknowledge him. He was counting heads. As quietly as he came he slipped away.

A short while later I saw the dean coming down the path, arms swinging purposefully in his military gait. He too stuck his head through the window. We exchanged nods, and he made a surprised face that made me grin. He went away to stand on the front steps. When the bell rang I went to join him.

"They're supposed to be on strike, you know," said the dean.

"But you saw them in class."

"You're the only teacher that has students in the whole department."

"Isn't that the way it's supposed to be?" He grinned. "Then there's nothing to worry about," I said. "I must get back." I left him scratching his head quizzically.

That morning, the entire junior class arrived. I was deeply moved. None of the other FE's classes were attended.

The dean was impressed. I was not concerned for myself, but for the students. Their absence during this time could weigh against them in the future.

Tuesday (25 April) passed in reasonable tranquility. But the city was tense. A student delegation tried to present their petition at the Great Hall but were not allowed in. They knelt on the steps, the petition held above their heads. It went on all day. When one collapsed another took his place.

Elsewhere, members of the State Council, the State Education Commission and the Beijing Municipal Committee of the Chinese Communist Party had agreed to a meeting with student representatives of Qinghua University. However the meeting did not take place. The *China Daily* report claims that the meeting failed to materialize because students could not agree on whom to send. The students claim that they did not attend because the state was not acting in good faith when it sent minor officials with no authority to speak for the government.

That night the government's official organ, *People's Daily*, published an editorial urging the people to stand firm against public disturbances, and announcing a ban on all further demonstrations. It stated that certain "outside influences" were using students' grief over the death of Hu Yaobang to disturb the stability of the state. Riots and looting had already taken place in Xian and Changsa and that such activities would not be tolerated. It also accused the same unnamed "outside influences" of fermenting opposition to the Communist party and the socialist system on campuses and using the names of workers' organizations to distribute reactionary pamphlets. It proclaimed the outlaw of autonomous organizations of teachers and students that have sprung up. "This is a planned conspiracy which, in essence, aims at negating the leadership of the Party and the socialist system," it went on to say. The editorial declared that the country was facing a grave political crisis which threatens its future. While affirming that the "students' sincere demands for the elimination of corruption and the promotion of democracy are also the demands of the Communist party and government," it left no doubt that further activity would be dealt with to the letter of the law.

The editorial was broadcast on radio and television. During the evening, loudspeakers were hooked up all over campus, and the strident message dinned upon us from all directions.

It roused a new wave of protest. Banners went up: "Patriotism is not a crime!" "Students are not criminals!" Cartoons appeared depicting Premier Li Peng in the uniform of the Nazi SS, and Deng Xiaoping as a lazy fat cat with a wine glass in one hand and a cigar in the other.

There was a huge rally on campus. Young men and women whom I have come to know quite well were transformed. I have never seen faces lit with such excitement and passion. A— has suddenly emerged as the student leader. A makeshift stage made of desks pushed together was set up in front of the boys' dorm. A— spoke at length with great passion. I was too far away to catch all that he said. But the response was tumultuous. A—'s slender handsome face was aglow with an inner fire—the kind of glow that might have lit the face of Joan of Arc following her voices. A—, the campus troubadour, had found his niche. God help him.

Watching those young faces around me, lit by torchlight singing "The Internationale," my hair stood on end.

> Arise, arise, you prisoners of starvation!
> Arise, you wretched of the earth!
> For justice thunders condemnation,
> A better world's in birth.
> No more tradition's chains shall bind us.
> Arise, you slaves, no more in thrall!
> The earth shall rise on new foundations,
> We have been naught, we shall be all . . .

I am not sure what this is all about anymore. In two weeks we have moved from mourning the death of a politician to something quite different. The issues have blurred in a welter of violence, rumors, and threats.

Y— suddenly emerged out of the gloom beside me. He smiled a shy greeting. "Do you understand what is happening?" I asked. He shook his head. "Nobody does," he said, "not even him." He pointed his chin at A— who was still speaking. "Then why is he up there?" Y— shook his head. "He's a performer," he said. That was too simple, and I would not accept it, particularly not from Y—, who is A—'s friend. "He's influenced by people at Bei Da, and the artist crowd he hangs out with. He thinks he knows what he's doing, but I doubt it." "And you?" Y— looked exhausted. "I've been sleeping in the classroom the last two weeks," he said, "just to get away from all the talk in the dormitory. I don't know how long I can stand it." The singing drowned out the rest of what he was saying.

> We want no condescending saviors,
> To rule us from a judgement hall;
> We workers ask not for their favors,
> Let us consult for all . . .

"What's going on?" I was almost yelling at Y—. "They're prepared to die," he said gripping my arm. "But it's none of your business. Take care." He walked away, his wide eyes gleaming.

There is something fatalistic in the Chinese psyche. They have a pathetically innocent and romantic view of martyrdom. It is as though the spilling of their blood is not only inevitable, but necessary and even desirable. They rush to their Golgotha without any notion what it is for. And if they don't know, who does? That is the tragedy.

The state has finally spoken. Yesterday Li Ximing, Party Secretary of the Beijing Municipal Committee of the Chinese Communist Party, briefed the city's 10,000 secretaries of the Party branches on the student demonstrations. An estimated 60,000 students out of 160,000 in 40 colleges and universities in Beijing had boycotted classes. Li accused them of stirring up turmoil with their big character posters and illegal unions, such as the Autonomous Union of Institutes of Higher Learning. He urged school administrations to take firm steps to put down any disturbances. He also warned that the state, ". . . will deal with them (student demonstrations) in accordance with the stipulation that no

demonstration is allowed without prior approval . . . "
Those are fighting words.

Today (27 April), the adminstration ordered the students
back to class. Tomorrow absentees will be strictly dealt
with. This morning there was a quiet, orderly sit-down
strike in front of the administration building. There were no
speeches, no songs. Silent, gaunt, hollow-eyed, hands linked
they sat in grim protest. The new slogan on the wall behind
them read: "Patriotism is not a crime. Students are not
criminals." The president, a scholarly man, spoke earnestly
and long, but it was no use. In 1976 when a spontaneous
eruption of poetry flooded the Square at the end of the
Cultural Revolution, he was a passionate writer. He was
also one of the intellectuals who helped in collecting and
editing that extraordinary outpouring for publication, one
of the scholars who gathered the poems that burst forth on
Tiananmen Square under the cry of "a hundred flowers
shall bloom." He was courageous and outspoken, and he
was admired. He became president of the institute and a bureaucrat. Many feel he has now become fat and complacent,
no longer the man he used to be. Nothing he said could
sway the students now.

At noon I watched the students march off with their
banners wearing white headbands with patriotic poems
written on them. I remember seeing young Japanese kami-
kaze pilots marching when I was still a child. The resemblance was startling and dreadful. Z—, who spotted me,
came over and shook hands. The others cheered "Long live
our foreign teacher!" We were both too choked for words.

(Later evening, 27 April) I broke off for awhile because
they were singing "The Internationale" again. Some of the
students who went to the Square were back. I saw J— in the
crowd and heaved a sigh of relief. But where were the others . . . so many others. There was to be a rally on the Square
and the students were bound to go. Rumor has it that armed
troops have already sealed off the University of Beijing,
People's University, and the access to the Square.

After the students dispersed I came back and turned on
the TV. The State Council has agreed to hear the student's

petition, provided it is presented through channels. Why this softening? Something terrible must have happened. The singing started again.

Sirens. A series of sharp pops like firecrackers. Silence.

It is past eleven and I am locked in the building. The silence is awful. I want to scream. O God, I have forgotten how to pray.

China is a sad country. Its problems are staggering. It tears at my heart. I want to leave it, yet I cannot bear the thought.

I shall stop here. In the morning I shall take this to the Beijing-Toronto Hotel and mail it there. I do not trust the local post office right now.

The institute is taking us on a trip to Mount Tai and the home of Confucius tomorrow. We shall be gone till next Tuesday. An ironic choice of destination, or is it judicious exile?

2

▶

Dear Mum,

It has been a worrisome time. But the worst seems to be over. The institute is far from the center of the disturbances. We were still affected to some degree but distance saved us from much of the grief. Foreigners are exceedingly vulnerable. Sooner or later they become scapegoats. The important thing is to appear neutral no matter where one's true sympathies lie.

Last weekend, at the height of the demonstrations, we were taken on a weekend tour to Qu Fu, the home of Confucius, and the sacred Mount Tai. It was wonderful to get away from the city, the smog, and the problems on campus. It was so quiet I could actually hear myself think again.

Quaint old Qu Fu is positively the cleanest place I've seen in China.

The Kung family, descendants of Confucius who account for one-third of the population of half a million, still has a strong influence on the life of the town. The Kungs agreed to a train station. But that is as far as they would go to modernize the town. The only forms of public transportation are brightly colored horse carriages. Six passengers face each other across an aisle. Once it gets going, you really have to hang on. The open-ended carriage tilts backward at a 45 degree angle, and you feel you are about to slide off. Nobody ever does. There are also sedan chairs, which make you sea-sick.

I did not realize how much I missed mountains until I

saw them on the horizon as the train left the plains. Mount Tai has fascinated me since I was a child. Some of the poetry about it I learned long ago has stayed with me. The mental picture I had was of dark craggy peaks, shrouded in cloud and mist; of ancient twisted pines, and birds. I had completely forgotten it was May Day and a public holiday. The crowds were enormous. The narrow flight of stone steps, cut into the mountain leading to the peak, was a Jacob's ladder. The mountain sides are quite heavily forested, so the view is restricted. All along the way there are small temples and shrines, and calligraphy both ancient and modern, carved into the living rock. There were poems by Li Bai and Tu Fu, calligraphy of emperors, and even a few lines by Mao hidden away in a small shrine. I enjoyed reading these inscriptions, which were lost on my companions, who were more interested in racing up the mountain.

The path is not difficult, but steep at times and the steps uneven. It took me four and a half hours to get to the top. I stopped frequently to look at a carving here and a shrine there, and to catch my breath. I am no longer in a hurry . The top of the mountain would make Confucius weep. When he stood on this peak centuries ago, he said the whole world could be seen from that spot. Twenty centuries later, Mao stood on the same spot. When he was asked his thoughts, he said, "The east is red."

Today's visitor sees the replica of a small Qing dynasty town, with several restaurants, a hotel and numerous antique and souvenir shops displaying American Express signs. There was a great din. Hawkers hawking, radios blaring, children screeching. Pickpockets were rife.

At the crest of the mountain there is an ancient temple. I nearly had my wallet lifted as I queued for a ticket to get in. I felt the wallet being lifted from my pocket, wheeled around and collared the young man behind me. Perhaps I reacted quicker than he expected, or he was hemmed in by the crowd and could not get away. I shook him till his teeth rattled, and he dropped the wallet. Afterwards, it was my turn to shake. I had become separated from my companions. There were three or four of them and one of me. So I hailed a policeman, who probably knew them anyway. It was a wise move. There was no more trouble after that, but I had lost interest in the temple. It was overcast, and the view was hidden under a blanket of cloud. Alas!

We were a group of thirty. Half were FEs and the rest were Russian students from the institute. I shared a compartment on the way back with three colleagues: Peter is German, Suzanne is French, and Nina is a Russian student. The only common language among the four of us was Chinese! The staff on the train thought four foreigners chattering at each other in Chinese was hilarious. Particularly when we resorted to charades when words failed us. Human communication is really a matter of willingness. Suzanne chain-smokes, and Peter is a fastidious non-smoker. His tirade on the evils of smoking which was three quarters pantomime and one quarter Chinese deserves to be filmed! But the point was made, and the French woman huffed out of the compartment and filled the corridor with smoke thereafter.

I have just finished my midterm exams. The semester is rapidly coming to an end. The juniors are gradually leaving for their practical work in travel agencies and hotels. The seniors will be writing their theses.

I shall be going home at the end of July. But I find it hard to turn my back on China. These have been two busy, exciting and productive years. I do not know what lies ahead. Now that all my sons are settled in their lives, my own ought to be fairly simple. I have stopped worrying about the future. So long as I have the peace and the energy to write and keep the wolf from the door I will be content. The same force that brought me back here will show me the direction when the time comes. Of that I am certain. All I need is patience.

9 May 1989   I'm still trying to learn to play the ancient Chinese chess game, Go. This afternoon J— and I went into town to buy a set. There are dozens of different kinds. Some made of bone, some of plastic, but the best are made of stone. There are 365 black and white pieces. The object of the game is to occupy as much of the board as possible.

J— is a good player. After a huge meal of spaghetti which we cooked, washed down with a very acceptable Chinese cabernet, we settled down to another lesson of Go.

"The board is an island," lectured J—. "We each mark out a territory we want to occupy, and the object is to secure and expand that territory." Sounds simple. But there are great heavy tomes written about the moves.

I kept getting pushed off the board, as usual. It was disgusting!

Each time I was beaten J— looked at me, expecting some display of temper. That's the way Chinese players react. When no display was forthcoming, he was puzzled.

"Are you not angry?" he asked. "Certainly not." He went over to the bookcase and poured us another brandy. "I think I'll hit you again," he said with a grin. That bit of slang has really taken root.

10 May 1989   There is a young man who is a ticket tout at the Beijing Concert Hall whom I've come to know. No matter what the weather is, he always wears a black leather jacket. Black Jacket pulls concert tickets out of the air, even when there are none to be had at the box office.

Tonight was a gala evening. The conductor was a Frenchman whose name I cannot decipher from the Chinese transliteration; the Central Philharmonic, and Chorus, plus four stars of the Central Opera. The program: Beethoven's Ninth.

I invited A— and J— to go with me. I had taken J— a few times before, but A— had never been to a symphony concert before and was a bit dubious. But he came along.

We found a hole-in-the-wall and ordered up a great plate of dumplings. A— insisted on buying a few cold dishes, and J— bought beer. There was plenty of time and we settled down to the serious business of food and drink. Suddenly there was only fifteen minutes to curtain time, and we hadn't got the tickets. We hurried to the concert hall; the dumplings and the beer were an uncomfortable mass in my stomach. The audience was already seated. The warning bell was going. We hurried across the plaza in front of the Concert Hall. There was no sign of Black Jacket.

"He's here! He's here!" I heard somebody shout, and sure enough Black Jacket was coming towards me, grinning from ear to ear, three tickets in hand.

"I saw you in the restaurant," he said, "so I kept these for you." "How did you know I didn't have tickets?" "You always eat before you buy tickets," he replied triumphantly. The man knows his clients.

I have heard the Ninth more times in Beijing than anywhere else.

It was a truly international performance. The conductor was French, the Chinese soloists sang in German, and the chorus in Chinese, but it came off very well.

By now J— has become an old hand at symphony concerts. I had introduced him to the Ninth some time ago, and he settled back to enjoy the music.

But it was all new to A—. He had never seen so many instruments, large and small. Oboes, clarinets, bassoons, flutes, violins, viola, cellos, timpani. I had to name them all and translate the names into Chinese. Aside from violins and cellos, I did not know any of the Chinese names for the other instruments. "And you don't like us to carry pocket dictionaries," A— scoffed, eyes twinkling. I had to admit one might have been handy just then. The light dimmed. The conductor emerged from the wings, and was given a rousing reception. He was a tall, thin man, whose arms seem to grow longer as the evening went on. A— sat bolt upright in his seat, eyes riveted to the stage. The conductor did not use a baton. His long fingers, probed, clutched, pulled the music out of the air. J—'s head nodded gently to the music. A small smile of recognition flitted across his face at familiar passages. A— was very pale even in the half light. The hand clutching the balcony rail trembled. Only when the last notes of the third movement faded into the upper darkness of the hall did he move.

The chorus filed in. The men in black evening clothes,

and the women in red robes. Then a wave of applause greeted the four soloists. The final movement began. As soon as the baritone came in, A— shot forward in his seat. He grasped J—'s hand excitedly, "I know that!" he whispered. J— whispered something to him. He turn around and smiled sheepishly. The chorus had begun the "Ode to Joy." The four solo voices weaved in and out of the huge fabric of chorus and orchestral sound higher and higher as though it would explode through the ceiling into the night sky. The drums rumbled, grew louder. And suddenly it was over.

A— slumped back into his seat, shaking as the audience roared its approval. The performers left the stage; the audience began to move toward the exits. We got up, each wrapped in his own thoughts. The Ninth touched me in a way it never had before.

The bus back to campus passed along the Square. I looked the other way. A— and J— stared out across it as we sped by. No one spoke.

17 May 1989

MY DEAR SONS,

A haunted silence has settled over the campus. The loudspeakers are no longer blaring. The buildings are empty. The foos are clustered around a TV in the lobby watching Gorbachev and Deng exchanging handshakes. They smile and smile. Deng resembles a wily old panda that could look tame one moment and claw you to death the next. There is something tentative, almost anxious in the way Deng clutches Gorbachev's sleeve for the final shot. It is the clawing grasp of a tired old man clinging to his page in history. This day's history is being made not far away, but well out of reach of TV cameras on the Square.

This is the fifth day of the students' hunger strike. The center of the city is once again cordoned off. In the last few days the hunger strikers have swelled from about 350 to several thousand. Today there will be more. The protest has become almost universal. Yesterday I went into the city and got as far as the perimeter of the square and no further. In the distance I could see the white banner of the institute. That is where my students were. I wanted to see them, but perhaps it was just as well that I could not. I have to remind myself constantly that I am a guest in a house where there is a quarrel. Although I know what is in my heart, I cannot—must not—be drawn in. For it will do no one any good. Yet it is very hard to be the bystander.

To make some sense of all this, I shall take up the story where I left off before.

Monday 1 May   Central and Beijing municipal officials met twice with student representatives. Afterwards Yuan Mu, the State Council spokesman, gave a press conference for foreign correspondents. The broadcast came on just as lunch was being served. The dining hall emptied within minutes. Everyone was huddled over the TV in their apartments.

Yuan Mu is a dour man whose long, deeply furrowed face, baggy eyes and gravelly voice betrays no emotion. He speaks in a heavily accented Mandarin, *putongha*, or common speech, as it is now called. The gist of his statement was that the state acknowledged the student movement was a non-subversive, spontaneous expression of concern for the country's well-being. The only note of levity in the proceedings was a mumbled reference to his personal income and those of his colleagues who were present which the interpreter failed to translate. There was a ripple of laughter and spattering of applause. But amid the seemingly conciliatory phrasing there was an ominous undercurrent. Looking straight into the camera, Yuan Mu reiterated time and again that "outside influences" were using the students to disturb the stability of the state. When members of the foreign press asked who these outside influences were, he would not say. However, the name of Fang Lizhi, the dissident astrophysicist, came up in a number of rhetorical questions. What were his intentions in criticizing the government? Who was in the background egging him on? Was he connected to some foreign power? Yuan was not prepared to elaborate on those questions as it would not be to the advantage of the government. On the question of recognizing the autonomous student organizations that have been formed, the answer was a definite and resounding "No." The government's position was that a state-sponsored student organization already existed and did a good job. There was, therefore, no need for any more.

On the note that further dialogues would be arranged in due course, the press conference ended.

Most people took the press conference at face value and thought it was a step in the right direction. Perhaps it was. *China Daily*, in reporting the event, also quoted the euphoric reactions of a handful of intellectuals who had participated in the student movement of May 4, 1919. Playwright and critic Xia Yen, now 89, who was active in the anti-feudalism movement seven decades ago, said that the May 4 Movement was a watershed between the new and the old democratic revolution. However, he conceded, democracy could not take root in a feudal society, or develop among illiterates. He pointed out that the May 4 movement failed to advocate establishing a legal system, which he believes essential for the development of democracy and science. Therefore, he believes, compulsory education and the development of a legal system must be pursued.

Wang Dezhao, a member of the China Academy of Sciences believes that the problem of improved funding for education, and teacher salaries, and the quality of education are paramount. Now 84, Wang states that the May 4 movement shaped the lives of youth of his generation. However, today's youth, faced with blatant corruption and no strong social ideology to bolster them, act on impulse.

The one thing that rattles around in my mind is Yuan Mu's statement that unnamed "outside forces" are using the students to ferment social upheaval. The state is looking for a scapegoat. Every foreigner has been put on notice. It is the oldest, most effective tool for terror. J—'s warning the last time we met, "You must be careful," made a lot of sense.

Campus settled down. Classes resumed but it was hard to get on with the work. The students who came were wan and hollow-eyed. Their minds were elsewhere. There were more empty seats than before. It did no good to ask where the absent ones were or what they were doing. The answer was always the same. "They are in the dormitory." A gulf separated us where none existed before.

One could sense something was brewing without knowing what it was.

Ironically, the Asian Development Bank is holding its annual meeting here right now. China is trying for a rather large loan, and is anxious to put its best foot forward. Perhaps that would keep things calm.

Wednesday 3 May   The students presented another ten-point petition and demanded a response by noon today or they would take to the streets again. The main thrust of the petition was that they be represented by their unregistered Autonomous Union of Beijing Colleges and Universities instead of the government-sponsored student federations in the dialogues with government. The students also insisted on speaking with government as equals, and having the right to choose which officials should attend.

The state rejected their demands in a special TV broadcast.

Campus was unusually quiet after the broadcast. A basketball tournament was played on schedule. That night the club was jammed for a double feature of kung-fu movies. G—, a bookish young man in his junior year who sat with me through the first of the punch-and-kick epics, said the movement was over. There was dissension among the students, between members of the recognized federation and the disallowed union. Sighed he, "Nobody knows what they are doing."

These days I find myself torn between two forces. On the one hand government, in spite of its faults, must preserve some semblance of stability. On the other hand the voice of the people also must be heard. The sad part of it is that the responsibility has been thrust upon inexperienced young people without any support. I hope this will end before things get out of hand and people get hurt.

Thursday 4 May   The seventieth anniversary of the May Fourth Movement. In1919, students took to the streets of Beijing to protest foreign invasion (Japan had seized Shandong province), demand democracy and revival of national pride.

Ten thousand students paraded around the Square this afternoon. Although the public security announced the rally was illegal since the organizers did not apply for permission, the police did not interfere. Maybe because the Asian Development Bank was meeting just a stone's throw away, the police that lined the streets around the square were unarmed. The students linked arms and marched in silence, holding up huge banners. "SUPPORT SOCIALISM AND REFORM." "LONG LIVE THE SPIRIT OF MAY 4TH." "GIVE US HUMAN RIGHTS." "OPPOSE OFFICIAL PROFITEERING." "THE MEDIA MUST TELL THE TRUTH." "HELLO, MR. DEMOCRACY." Students from other cities joined the rally. There were banners identifying major universities in Tianjin, Shanghai, Nanjing, Wuhan, Changchun and even Hong Kong. For the first time journalists were among the protestors. The only sound above the marching feet was the breaking of hundreds of small bottles. Here the Chinese love of puns comes into play. Deng's name, *Xiaoping*, has the same sound as the words meaning "small bottle." Only five years ago at the national day rally people held up a banner that read "GREETINGS, XIAOPING!" Today's bottle smashing must surely be a measure of disillusionment.

It was impressive.

Riding the Chinese faculty bus into town in the afternoon, I listened to the comments of some teachers. The consensus was the students were out on a lark. One cynical older man sneered, "Conditions are different from 1919. What do they know about patriotism?" Yet the students are demanding better conditions for people like him!

After the rally the students announced they would resume classes the next day.

Once again, peace and normalcy. The posters all over campus disappeared overnight. The blare of rock-and-roll replaced the shrilling of weeks passed. The students are emotionally and physically exhausted. Half of one junior class appeared this morning. Their practicum has been advanced, and they were packing to leave for Guanzhou and Wuhan tomorrow. I bade them farewell and dismissed them. The second class did not appear at all. They had already been sent off, and the third class was leaving this afternoon. The institute is trying to put them out of harm's way by sending them off a month ahead of schedule. I wish them well. My only regret is that I did not have a chance to bid them farewell and take a class photo.

Students go through the motions of their daily lives, but they have changed imperceptibly. Their naiveté (Chinese students in their early twenties are far more naive than their Canadian or U.S. counterparts) has been demolished. In its place is an indescribable weariness and sadness. J— said to me that China has not changed, and will never change. Feudalism lives on under a different guise. Even the imperial system continues though the title is not the same. And it's true. One poster on campus listed the names of all members of government and their titles. It was a veritable family tree of the Dengs, the Zhaos and the Lis. As the Chinese put it, "Old wine in new bottles."

Tuesday 9 May   A petition signed by Beijing journalists was presented to the All-China Journalists Association demanding freedom of the press and fair reporting of current events. The journalists cited the less than objective reporting of the student demonstrations, and the dismissal of the chief editor of the Shanghai-based *World Economic Herald* for an editorial that was critical of the current situation. Students of several universities went out in support of the journalists.

The loudspeakers are blaring again, and "The Internationale" is once again tearing my guts out. The movement has risen to a different plane. There is more to come.

Wednesday 10 May   My classroom hours are down to two hours a week with the seniors now that the juniors are gone. It was not until the afternoon when I had done the day's writing, and got on the Chinese faculty's bus to town that I noticed how quiet the campus was. There was hardly a bicycle in sight.

The Chinese faculty members have their own axes to grind just now. The new faculty flats are ready for occupancy, but who is allocated what is the burning question. As the game of musical flats goes on, faculty feathers are flying. That students are once more boycotting classes becomes a matter of no concern.

The bus came to a screeching halt several miles from the city center. A steady stream of bicycles went by. The riders rode six abreast, hands clasped on each other's shoulders. There were banners of half a dozen newspapers and wire services, as well as universities. The silent procession went on and on. There was a sprinkling of foreigners among them. Mostly young women trailing long colored scarves riding pillion behind young Chinese men, obviously out for a lark. Fools who invariably stir up trouble, albeit unwittingly.

Saturday 13 May   About 350 students went on hunger strike this afternoon, protesting government procrastination in resuming talks. There are so many rumors that one does not know what to believe.

Coming home from a concert this evening I encountered B—. B— is a charismatic young man who speaks English liberally spiced with American slang. He said he had been to a banquet for classmates who were joining the hunger strike tomorrow. I asked if he was joining too. B— smiled. "Not a chance. I've got plans," he said. B— is tour-guiding whenever he can and hoarding his tips in FEC for a passport and visa to America. "Are there tourists?" I asked. B— shrugged. "A few. They're curious." He had been drinking white lightning and beer and he wanted to talk about the banquet. "It was our teachers' treat," he said. "It was a kind of send off, you dig? Some of the poor jerks are prepared to die. They've even made out wills." He patted the breast pocket of his jacket. He prattled on about the food. My mind wandered. It was more than I could comprehend. I won't try. "Gorbachev is coming soon," remarked B—. I commented that it was poor timing for the hunger strike. It would cause a serious loss of face for the government, which is bound to retaliate. "Nonsense. They wouldn't dare," said B—, completely sure of himself. I do not share his optimism.

Sunday 14 May   The second day of the hunger strike. The number of fasting students has grown to over a thousand. The city is tense, as tomorrow Gorbachev arrives for the summit. In the afternoon members of government met with the students. Two points were raised. The students asked that the talks be broadcast live for the hunger strikers, and that the government admit the demonstrations have been a patriotic movement. Although the government spokesman appeared friendly, both requests were denied, and the talks were recessed. J— and I watched the proceedings on the TV. We talked for a long time afterward. The romantic idea of martyrdom which even J— harbors frightens me. These students are willing to die before they have begun to live.

Monday 15 May   The third day of the hunger strike. The days are blazing hot, but the temperature drops considerably at night. The strikers are out in the open. The smog stings the eyes and burns the lungs. Over half of the original group have collapsed and been taken to hospital. It is not surprising. They already suffered from malnutrition. On top of it many have refused water as well.

But more keep pouring into the Square. Gorbachev's state welcome had to be moved to the airport. Soldiers ringed the Great Hall. The striking students moved in waves up the steps of the Great Hall and the soldiers pushed them back, but the tide surged forward again. It went on like that for hours, but there was no violence.

Tuesday 16 May   The fourth day of the hunger strike. Many academics, writers, journalists and teachers have joined ranks with the students. The center of the city is cordoned off. But there are no police or soldiers on the Square. One hunger striker collapses every six minutes now. Several first-aid tents have been set up, and sirens are going all the time. A doctor has warned that the heat and smog are dangerous to the fasting students. The International Red Cross has appealed for portable toilets and opening fire hydrants for water. The sanitary conditions on the Square have been called extremely dangerous to public health. One spokesperson warned that the city could face a serious epidemic of hepatitis and cholera if this situation is allowed to continue much longer.

And so we come to this haunted campus. This morning the president, who had toed the Party line till now, mobilized the school buses and led the students and faculty to the square. Foreigners were excluded. I watched them go. Silent, orderly, determined. I wanted to cheer and I wanted to cry. This thing has become nationwide. It is not only the intelligensia now. Factory workers and even party members have joined. I do not know where it will end. No one can tell. So long as Gorbachev is here I think everything will be calm though a million people are marching through the streets in the center of the city. Tomorrow it may be different. I am going to try and reach my students on hunger strike with a backpack of juice. I don' t know if I'll get through but I must try.

Part Three

The Storm Breaks

Part Three

The Short Trials

1

▶

15 May 1989   I am terribly restless. My classes have stopped. This morning I walked into an empty classroom. None of the seniors appeared. I sat in the shabby room alone and angry. The walls could do with a good coat of paint. The desks need new tops. Some of the seats were empty metal frames. But there are no graffiti anywhere. It is a sad room when all the people are gone. The dust motes dance in the sunlight, and the green shadows of trees flicker across the walls. After a while I gathered up my things and headed for the dean's office. He was not there, but the political leader was in.

C— was most apologetic. "The seniors have two weeks off for their thesis. Someone should have told you." "Well no one did. Then they come back on June 1?" "Then they have two weeks to defend their thesis, and after that it's finals." "In other words, I have no more classes." "That's right," smiled C—. "Have a good rest. Go traveling." Go traveling? Pieter, Helen and I had been planning a weekend in Inner Mongolia to see the ancient monastery of Wudangzhou for months. Now, Pieter can't go. Helen is a pleasant, dithery woman. A poet whom I cannot really fathom. At times she is a left over flower-child of the '60s, liberated, easygoing. At other times she is the starchy, prissy schoolmarm. I've seen her tossing off beer like it was going out of style, and been with her when she wouldn't let a drop past her lips. Helen is a contradiction, and I don't know whether I want to cope with her alone.

16 May 1989   Helen is quite determined to go to Wu-dangzhou and I agreed to make the air reservation. N—, who was having tea with me when she called yesterday afternoon, insisted that she would get her assistant, who has connections with CACA, to make the reservations.

"You will waste time and energy trying to do it yourself," she assured me. Much as I detest going through "the back door" as they call it, I agreed. When in China, do as the Chinese. Her eyes went wide when she realized the friend I was going with is a woman. I carefully explained she is English and a Foreign Expert at another college. I could tell N— was not pleased. Although she has been abroad, and is a modern woman in every sense, the thought of a man and woman traveling together conjures up a rumpled bed. I did not explain. It would only make things worse.

N—'s assistant was as good as her word. The reservation was confirmed the same evening.

I arranged to meet Helen at the CACA ticket office near Beihai Park this afternoon to pick up the tickets. The CACA office for international flights was practically empty. There were a few foreigners haggling with the clerks, filling in endless forms. The domestic flight section was mobbed. I looked everywhere for Helen, but could not find her. I walked back to the street and waited at the bus stop for a while, and went back to CACA again. The crowd was getting thicker. There was even a crush at the wicket that was clearly marked "Foreigners Only."

A fist-fight had broken out between an irate customer and a ticket clerk who was accused of giving the customer's seat to another person. Although the combatants had been restrained by public security, they were still snarling at each other, and the bystanders were egging the customer on. Clearly there had been sculduggery on the part of the ticket clerk.

When the dust finally settled, the ticket clerk was in high dudgeon. One eye was slowly blackening, and the side of her face was puffing up. "There are two people on the file," she said, mispronouncing the names painfully. I explained that I was buying my ticket only. The other person was on her way. "But I will have to separate the file," she complained. I apologized for being a nuisance, but since she could not sell me Helen's ticket without seeing her passport, that is what she would have to do. She glared at me balefully, but she did what she had to do, and I got my ticket.

Later, Helen called. She had tried to reach the CACA office by taxi from the Friendship Hotel where she lives. But Changan Street was blocked several kilometers west of the Square. Nor could she get through by circling northward. In the end, she went back to the hotel. But her English dander was up.

"We're definitely going," she said in her crisp English schoolmarm voice.

The trip is getting off to a flying start.

17 May 1989 The school administration has had a complete change of heart regarding the student movement. The scholarly president of the institute was dead set against it at the start. He did everything from cozy chats to angry harangues to get the students back into the classrooms. But he failed. Some of the young teachers now openly support the students. But there are many more like young Siu who pull a long face, and whine about the need to clean up corruption and improve education, but are content to leave the dirty work to someone else. Now the president has swung around to supporting the students. Perhaps the reminders of his younger years that the students have been flinging in his face finally got to him. More likely it was the way he reads the winds of change that prompted his impassioned open letter to the government in support of the hunger strikers. When a poster of the letter appeared on a bulletin board this morning, the Chinese faculty was quick to endorse it, almost to a man. Even some of the most rabid party members signed.

The campus exploded with such joy and solidarity that

it became a different place overnight. The ghetto-blasters were blaring rock-and-roll. People were rushing about everywhere, smiling, chattering, excited. Strangers came up to me, hugged and shook my hand, and thumped me on the back. The institute's fleet of buses were quickly organized to carry students and Chinese faculty to the Square for a mass rally. I watched the buses leave campus, banners waving. "The Internationale" rang across the campus:

> To make the thief disgorge his booty,
> To free the spirit from the cell,
> We must ourselves decide our duty,
> We must decide and do it well.

It was no longer just the voice of youth raised in defiant song. Intermingled was the voice of experience whose conscience had been pricked.

I wandered back to my apartment. Every fiber in my body was alive. A long hot shower later I still tingled with excitement. I wanted to be out there. But I could not be. I was alone and marooned.

A fierce thunderstorm blew up just after dark. For an hour it poured and the thunder rattled the sky. J— arrived drenched, shivering and bedraggled, but happy, bursting with excitement, and hungry. I got some dry clothes and shoved him into the shower. All I had was eggs, bread, and milk. I made a stack of French toast, and J— wolfed it, babbling excitedly between mouthfuls.

The strikers on the Square remained at their posts. The marchers continued without changing their pace. Finally the rain stopped.

Thursday, 18 May   The day dawned, dark and windy. Classes have been suspended again. The air crackled with excitement. There was a great deal of shouting and running about. The campus was a hornet's nest gone mad. At midday N— came for lunch. J— told me A— and some others of their grade were fasting on the Square. "They need juices to keep their strength up," he had said. The idea of doing something for the students has been brewing at the back of my mind for days. Although I will not sign petitions or march, I felt I could do something personal, on a humanitarian basis. There was to be another bus for a teachers' rally in the afternoon. It was the only way I could get to the Square, as public transportation had stopped. N— was going and I asked if I could go along. At first the administration's answer was "no." Later they changed their mind. They figured I would not be too conspicuous, if I promised to blend with the crowd. I rushed to the tuck shop, slammed my backpack on the counter and told the bewildered old man to fill it with cartons of fruit juice. The man was flabbergasted. I kept saying, "Hurry, hurry," and he kept putting them in. He was even more surprised when I paid him and said thank you.

It was a long bus, and it was already packed to the gunwales. A thin, mousey little girl from the senior class was scrambling on ahead of me. She was one of the quiet ones that never says a word, and while I recognized her, I did not know her name. She offered to carry the pack for me, but I would not hear of it. We clambered onto the bus, and lurched out of campus.

The south road was clogged. There were truckloads of workers from various factories carrying banners and slogans, and peasants on bicycles all streaming toward the Square. People lined the streets, cheering and giving us the V-for-Victory sign. On the bus faculty and students mingled with a wonderful feeling of solidarity. There were several retired professors and their wives who looked too frail to stand the ride into town, but were determined to march in the rally.

People were coming from everywhere. On foot, by bicycle. The public buses stopped at a place called Bawangfen (Tomb of Eight Princes). From there on, the school bus inched forward, hemmed in by a moving stream of humanity. But it was orderly, and surprisingly quiet. The demonstrations seemed to have drawn people closer to one another. They smile, and greet each other with a *"Ni hao,"* though they may never rub shoulders again.

The bus could not go beyond the overpass at Jianguomen. Everybody spilled out. A huge banner, "FACULTY AND STAFF OF THE INSTITUTE SUPPORT THEIR HUNGER STRIKERS," led our contingent. Smaller banners identifying each faculty followed. We fell in ten abreast behind the banner of our respective departments. Hands linked, we moved into Changan Street, then turned west toward the Square. Each institution's contingent was marked off by white ropes. I have never been in the midst of such a crowd before. A million people marched. The barriers of age, caste, and politics disappeared. An unspoken bond was forged through our linked hands. I became part of a vast family. I belonged.

The skinny little girl had literally torn the pack off my back when I got off the bus and bolted into the crowd with it. I knew it would be safe, but I wanted to deliver it myself. Besides, it was heavy. I kept breaking ranks and running ahead, trying to find her. But she had disappeared.

This rally was different from the others. Besides students and teachers, there were also workers from hotels and offices along the route, and two-thirds the staff of Capital Steel Works, the largest industrial employer in the city. There was even a truckload of off-duty policemen who had really gone out on a limb to support the students.

Banners and posters were everywhere. One particularly poignant one was of a huge eye and a single teardrop. Deng was again caricatured as a lazy fat cat, with the slogan, "A GOOD CAT KNOWS WHEN TO LEAVE." "OLD DENG YOU CAN GO NOW." "READ CHINA DAILY! READ BETWEEN THE LIES!" proclaimed a huge banner in English held up by journalists. The hotels and the office towers were festooned with streamers that read: "SUPPORT THE STUDENTS; PATRIOTISM IS NOT A CRIME."

Old icons of the Cultural Revolution were dusted off and brought out again. There were many posters of Mao and Zhou Enlai. Was this turning into a replay of the Cultural Revolution?

"It's nostalgia," said N— walking beside me, but her grip on my hand tightened. "People are thinking back to the early days. Life was tough but the leaders were clean . . ."

The sidewalks were filled with people, laughing and

cheering us on. I was on the edge of the marchers, close to the sidewalk. A few peered at me, scratched their heads, and remarked, "Was that a *lao wai?*" meaning "old foreigner." There were many people with cameras, and a few were pointed in my face. It was hard to avoid being photographed. Every time a camera was pointed in my direction my heart lurched. But there was nothing I could do except brazen it out.

Lightning rippled through the lowering sky. The air was dense and heavy. The only sound was the tramp of a million feet, punctuated by slogans shouted from somewhere among the marchers and answered by the throng on the sidewalks.

A wind came up from nowhere snapping the banners and placards, and shaking the trees along Changan Street. Halfway to the Square it began to rain. Big, lazy drops grew thicker and harder, until it pounded down. Thunder rocked the sky. Someone nearby remarked, "Even the heavens are angry!" We walked on at the same measured pace. People jamming the sidewalks thrust umbrellas at us, and sheets of cardboard. Although N— had a small umbrella, it was not much help. The wind churned the rain into a whirling dervish.

As we neared the Square, the rain suddenly let up. Watery sunlight pushed through the clouds. People laughed and cheered. There was a great feeling of warmth; of shared experience and aspirations. Near the Square, a peasant, stripped to the waist, was perched atop one of the ancient pines,

"Long live the students! Long live the teachers!" he cheered.

And the people on the sidewalk cheered with him. I was anxious about the backpack. Delivering the juice to my fasting students was the main purpose of the exercise. I ran along the column straining for the skinny girl, when I spotted a boy with wine-red pack. It was mine. The pack had been passed from one person to another. I thanked the boy and strapped it on. I did not realize how heavy it was.

Only when we reached the Square did I discover I would never get near the hunger strikers. Eight traffic lanes filled with marchers separated me from the Square itself. We were going right past the Square and I would not be able to reach my students.

It was a day when things happened. Suddenly B—, a junior, appeared beside me.

"What are you doing here?" B— flashed me a surprised grin.

B— had been sleeping on the Square. Two nights earlier, I was trying to persuade him to stay away from the Square at night. The Square at night fills me with a nameless dread. Even as he promised he would stay away, I knew he would be there the next night.

I told B— my errand.

"I'll take you to our students," he said.

B— is tall, slender and handsome, crowned with a mop of unruly curly hair. He is the only student who comes to class in a suit and tie. He speaks English well enough to pass for a Hong Kongite. Today he was almost unrecognizable. The suit was replaced by a red T-shirt, black gym pants, and white runners. A red bandana was tied around his head. There was a pretty girl in a black jumpsuit with him. I left the marchers and peeled off with the two young people. We ducked through an underpass and came up on the Square.

Ninety buses were ranged along the north end of the Square where the hunger strikers were. The long search began. We went from bus to bus asking for students of the institute. We peered at the shrunken faces of young men and women who looked old beyond their years. We stopped people, talked with harried Red Cross nurses tottering from the heat, the fetid air and fatigue. Finally, someone suggested they might still be out in the open. B— knew the campsite was at the foot of the monument facing the Forbidden City. We pushed through the throng, and came against the first of many obstacles. The students had formed a human chain to keep access open for the ambulances that came and went constantly, carrying strikers who had collapsed to hospital. No one was allowed to pass. We pressed on southward. Eventually we came to a break in the link and darted across the open space. We were within reach of the campsite, when a pair of hands seized me from behind. We were ordered back.

"He's our foreign teacher," explained B—," and he has fruit juice for our strikers."

The young man who held me by the straps of my backpack scrutinized me.

"If I let you through, you might not be able to leave," he warned.

"I'll worry about that later," said I.

"All right," he said, after a moment's thought," I'll let you through. But you mustn't stay. It may not be safe."

I thanked him and we pushed on.

We found them at the foot of the monument just as B— said we would, huddled under a sheet of wet plastic that was beginning to steam. A—, the leader, sat cross-legged on the ground strumming his guitar singing, "Where have all the flowers gone . . . ?" The others joined in feebly. There were about twenty of them. Perhaps more. Most were too exhausted to sing, and just lay in the wet, among the heaps of garbage and bottle shards. Their faces were ashen; the bones pressed outward under the translucent skin. Black, fathomless eyes gazed into the distance, devoid of all emotion. There was neither anger, hope, nor despair. They gazed at death. A void. I did not realize until then the dreadful implication of that void to people without religion; for whom there was no notion of heaven and hell, or even rebirth. For them, death is truly the end. Yet they were unflinching, resigned, ready. It took A— a moment to recognize me. Then we were hugging and laughing together. The others who were not too weak to move swarmed around me. I distributed the cartons of juice, and helped the weak ones to drink. They all wore red headbands, with patriotic verses written on them. Red is the color of martyrdom. One by one they brought their headbands and asked me to sign them. A—, intense and passionate . . . O—, always too timid to speak . . . M—, serenely knitting even here . . . Y—, the young librarian who has circumnavigated the globe in books . . . D—, who was never more than skin and bone, leaned against my shoulder making gurgling sounds that passed for speech. These students who are so poorly nourished were reduced to nothing. I had gone to try and alleviate some of their suffering. Instead, they were valiantly trying to cheer me.

"Sing us a song teacher!"

I shook my head. My mind was mush, and I did not trust my voice.

"We'll sing," said A—, and launched into "Blowing in the Wind."

B— tugged at my elbow and gestured it was time to go. I laid D— down and slipped a pile of rags under his head. He smiled with that faraway look in his eyes that froze my heart. A— and the others hugged me, and once more, clasping hands with B— and the girl, we pressed northward past the Mausoleum to Qianmen Street.

Qianmen Street, the southern border of the Square, was lined three deep with soldiers. They carried no arms. The crowds were thinner.

B— said, "I have to leave you now." We shook hands all around. He and the girl disappeared in the crowd.

I pushed myself across the street and walked the five or six blocks to N—'s apartment. Although I still squished in my shoes, my clothes were beginning to dry and to stink. N— was not yet home. Her granddaughter poured me a stiff drink of white lightning. Presently, N— appeared, tired, bedraggled but smiling.

"You made it?"

"Yes."

"And?"

"It was all right." One learns to use few words. She nodded. After she had washed and changed, and we had eaten, I made my way home.

The subway station nearby was barred and padlocked. I walked to the Beijing-Toronto Hotel about two miles away, but the taxis were not moving. I walked on. At the edge of town the road was barricaded by buses and trucks. People were tearing up road dividers with their bare hands and old women with bound feet were piling bricks by the wayside. There was a rumor that the army was coming. A farmer with a flat-decked tricycle spotted my red faculty pin and hailed me. "Teacher, I'll give you a ride."

"My institute is far away, " I said.

"Just tell me where you're going," he said. He shoved a stick with a white cloth tied to it in my hand, on which a few characters had been scrawled.

"Just hold it up, and we'll get through," he said.

I did as I was told. We took off down the road. The white flag and my red pin got us through the road blocks.

I have washed off the sweat and the dust, and taken a stiff belt of Scotch. I am drowsy.

A—'s voice keeps sounding in my head:

> Where have all the flowers gone?
> Young girls picked them every one,
> When will they ever learn,
> When will they ever learn?

19 May 1989   I woke with a headache. The maid came for the first time in a week. For the first time since I have been here the big bright smile, which I have come to expect was missing. She worked in silence.

"Is your mother-in-law all right?" I asked. The old woman had been ill.

"Yes," she answered almost shortly, then added, "I haven't been able to get to work for a week."

I said I understood. There was another silence. Then she suddenly exploded with a tirade against the old men who had a strangle hold on the nation. I listened in silence. I trust the woman implicitly, but . . .

The phone rang. There was a querulous note in Helen's voice. "Are you still game for Inner Mongolia?" I was not sure. Half of me wanted desperately to be away from Beijing, away from the silent campus, away from all the disturbing events that threatened to engulf me if I let them. The other half felt almost compelled to stay.

Aloud I said, "I'm game," though without much conviction.

"You're sure?" Helen can be perceptive at times.

"I am," I said, this time quite firmly.

We arranged to meet in the lobby of the Great Wall Hotel at two. That would give us ample time to reach the airport for a five o'clock flight to Baotou.

A quick call to the embassy produced very little that was enlightening.

"We think it's quite safe to travel," the voice said glibly. "Just keep away from crowds." I thanked him and hung up.

I rode the public bus as far as the Third Ring Road. From there on the road was clogged. The police had disappeared from the streets. Students were directing traffic and doing the best they could. I scrambled off the bus and continued on foot until I found a taxi idling by the wayside.

"I'll go if you pay FEC," said the driver and named his price.

The fare was ridiculous but it had taken more than an hour to get this far, and it was almost two o'clock. I agreed with reckless abandon. It's only money and funny money at that.

The flight that was supposed to be sold out was half empty. The propeller-driven aircraft lumbered over the mountains and leveled off across the barren yellow plains that eventually merged into the yellow sand dunes of Inner Mongolia.

Baotou is a strange divided city. The airport is near the old town; a random collection of tottering old buildings that look curiously European, and deep rutted dirt roads, where children and pigs wander. A belt of trees and gardens separate it from the new town forty-five kilometers away.

The Friendship Hotel bears the unmistakable traits of its Russian origins. We had no reservations.

"We have no singles left," said the disinterested desk clerk. However, after some persuading on my part, she came up with a twin, with bath attached. As Helen was agreeable—not that we had any choice; the alternative being a park bench—I said we'd take it.

There followed a bit of haggling over the price: FEC versus RMB. Our letters of introduction from the institute were grudgingly accepted after a supervisor was brought in. We filled the registration cards.

"Are you married?" the desk clerk asked. "No," said I straight-faced. The woman gasped in horror. "In that case, I'm not sure." "Not sure about what?" "About the propriety." Her eyes went from me to Helen and back again registering disapproval. "We're foreigners," I reminded her. "To us it doesn't matter." Another noisy intake of breath. We were obviously going to darken the name of the establishment. I waited. "It's only for one night," she mumbled. "Two," I corrected her. "Two nights." Her face clouded. I braced myself for new developments. "I suppose if you don't mind." "We don't." She shoved the key at me with a look of disgust on her face. "Do we pay now, or when we leave?" She thought a moment. "I'll think about it," she said momentously. "If I want the money in advance I'll come and fetch it."

The room was large and musty even with the windows wide open. The two narrow beds were lumpy. The bathroom was like a sauna. The hot water tap of the shower would not shut off. Where else would you find a rain storm indoors?

Half an hour later, we were having a cup of (instant) coffee when the door suddenly flew open. The desk clerk strode in with an armful of towels. "I brought you fresh towels," she chirped. I took them from her and ushered her through the door. "What was that about? We already have towels," remarked Helen. "She was inspecting us," I replied. "Inspecting?" "She expected to catch us in bed." "Oh." Helen had reverted to her starchy English schoolmarm mode.

After a meal of dumplings we wandered down the street. As we turned onto the main street a small procession was coming toward us. There could not have been more than a hundred students on bicycles, waving placards and shouting slogans. A few bystanders, mostly old people, watched sullenly from the sidewalk. After awhile we wandered back to the hotel.

2

▶

20 May 1989   I was wakened by a loud voice. I glanced at my watch; it was one o'clock. The voice was coming from a loudspeaker somewhere in the garden or the courtyard in front of the hotel. The echoes bounced off the three buildings and made nonsense of the words. But the voice was harsh, and without understanding any of the words I sensed something dire was happening. There were other sounds. Running footsteps; voices, probably the staff roused from their beds. The harangue seemed to go on a long time. The darkness distorted the sound and the passage of time so that both seemed interminable. At last it ended.

Helen slept like a log. I wish I had that ability to shut out the world around me when it did not suit me.

I could not find a news broadcast on the radio in the morning. The staff in the dining room whispered in little clusters. If they were uninterested in the guests the night before, we might just as well be invisible now. The waitress who brought our food spoke only Mongolian when I asked her the news. The night before, she had spoken Mandarin very well. Helen was oblivious to all this, and I thought it just as well to keep her in the dark, happily scanning the *Lonely Planet* book, and reading snippets to me about Wudangzhou.

After breakfast, while she packed, I went in search of a taxi to take us out into the desert and Wudangzhou Lamasery, and also to buy train tickets back to Beijing.

For once the CITS girl was cheerful and willing. All their tours have been canceled for the summer, and she was glad to have something to do rather than stare at the drab walls the rest of the day.

The Mongolian driver I finally settled on was an obliging fellow who piloted his own cab. He was in his early thirties, but looked closer to my age. Pleasant and sensible while immobile, he became a holy terror behind the wheel. We roared through the town narrowly missing cyclists and mule carts, bounced across the railway tracks in front of an oncoming train, squealed around hairpin turns inches from the edge of yawning gorges, talking a blue streak all the while.

"What is he saying?" Helen shrieked over the roar of the engine. The taxi had no muffler. "Li Peng has declared martial law." "When?" yelled Helen. There was a strange unfocused look in her eyes. "At 1 A.M." We rode a while in silence. The driver had given me all the news and subsided into silence. The crunch was coming. I looked up at the sky, white with the heat of noon, half expecting the Big Foot to hover there.

Wudangzhou floated into view, shimmering in the heat eddies, suspended like a mirage above the surrounding dunes. The guidebooks compare it to the Potala, but it is nowhere as large or imposing. Wudangzhou is an oasis of tranquility nestled among the golden, yellow dunes. A few ancient lamas with blackened teeth and gummy eyes collected our money and let us in the various halls. Inside, it was dark and cool. The crumbling structures had not been restored in hundreds of years. The dusty, deserted halls were blackened by candle smoke and permeated with the indefinable sweetness of incense. Every inch of wall was covered with frescoes. Most were overlaid with so much grime that only a faint suggestion of their splendor shone through. But where they were far from the altars, the colors remained fresh and vibrant.

I had asked the driver to listen to the news for me. But there was nothing new.

In the evening, Li Peng's speech from the Great Hall was

rebroadcast. This doughy, bland-looking man spoke in an emotionless monotone. Again, the accusing finger was pointed at the anonymous few working behind the scenes using the students as a means of overthrowing the government. Li urged an end to the hunger strike, and resumption of classes on all campuses. The speech was a masterpiece of double-talk. While he reiterated several times that the students' actions were an expression of patriotic fervor, he also hinted that they were counterrevolutionaries bent on destroying the regime. Only once did his voice change pitch, when he called the students anti-revolutionaries, and demanded they be put down. The army was being brought into the capital for the safety of the people, he said; to protect and not to bear arms against them.

Yang Shangkun, the president, was next to speak. In a halting, lugubrious voice he repeated what Li had already said. His speech ended lamely. "The army loves the people . . . the army loves the people . . . the army loves the people . . . " Either he had lost the script, or the springs that kept him going were winding down. The camera panned across the capacity audience in the Great Hall. Cadres of the Party, government, and army were all there. Most were incredibly old. Many were slumped in their seats, asleep. Others gaped with their mouths open, uncomprehending. It was frightening to think that a billion people's lives were manipulated by this collection of fossils.

Sometimes not knowing a language is a blessing. Helen slept as peacefully as a child. I lay awake a long time after the lights were turned off. The various telecasts of the past few days flashed through my mind. All the top brass were there last night except Deng, Zhao Ziyang and Hu Qili.

In the last few days Zhao has emerged as a moderate. He is an astute man and a survivor. First there was his controversial and highly publicized statement to Gorbachev on national television that Deng was consulted on all major issues. In fact, Deng was the real power in China. The revelation that the nation had been duped two years ago into believing Deng had relinquished all his political power exploded like a bombshell. Then there was the late-night visit to the hunger strikers on the Square and in the hospitals in which he openly lauded the students for their patriotism, urged them to end their fast and live for the fruition of their cause.

Li had been less sympathetically visible. A televised dialogue with the student leaders Wang Dan and Wu'er Kaixi ended in a deadlock. The student leaders had gone from their hunger strike. Wang Dan was so weak that he had to be given oxygen during the talk. It was a clash of implacable wills from the start. There is a difference between arrogance and determination. The students' demand that government recognize their movement as patriotic was a reasonable one. But the way in which it was presented was arrogant. The delicate business of protocol and face-saving was totally disregarded. Li's back was up, and he exploded in a furious tirade which was flashed simultaneously across the TV screens across the nation. It showed the man for what he is. He was his bland, expressionless self again on his nocturnal visit to the hunger strikers. In the hospital he sat on the edge of a young man's bed and listened to what he had to say. The young fellow looked about nineteen, but was probably older. He was articulate and passionate. He began by saying that the Communist party's contributions to the country were undeniable. The student movement was not aimed at overthrowing it, but to point out areas where attention was urgently required. He named four points: the chaotic condition of the economy; the misuse of natural resources and the squandering of human resources; the need for better education; and freedom of the press. He ended by saying that although not all officials are corrupt, many did profit from their positions. He urged them to put their house in order and then do the same for the nation. It was a courageous speech.

Hu Qili, the propaganda chief and Zhao's protegé, kept well out of range of microphones.

In light of all this, it was not surprising that Zhao was not present when martial law was announced. His star had been fading for some time. But the revelation of Deng's continuing role in government, and Zhao's tearful remarks when he visited the students on the Square, "Alas, we have come too late," probably presages the end of his career.

21 May 1989   The platform at Baoto Station where we waited for the train to Beijing was crowded with uniformed men. There was a mixture of uniforms. The old baggy ones with no insignias; and the smart, new, fitted ones with stripes on the sleeves and pips in the collars. It is still hard to tell who is what. The girl at CITS managed two soft berths for us. I slept badly the night before and was very tired. Helen had retreated into her English schoolmarm role, with her nose buried firmly in her book.

I clambered onto the upper berth and stretched out. We were the only foreigners on the train. Once they were on board, the uniforms disappeared. On the train, everyone was a civilian. Just before we pulled out, a burly fellow with a large paunch came in and sat down. A few moments later he was joined by a square-faced man with a briefcase. Although they were both in civilian clothes, they had a military bearing. They did not seem to know each other. But I could not be sure.

"Who are they?" asked Helen in her prim English voice. "I don't know. Probably watchdogs." "But, foreigners are supposed to be . . . " Helen commenced to splutter. "They probably understand," I said rather curtly. "Be quiet." Helen looked hurt. The man with the briefcase looked at us speculatively. I am sure he understood English

As the train picked up speed, the two men settled down. Cigarettes were passed between them, and introductions were made. The fat man was from Shandong, and the square-faced man with the briefcase was from the northeast. They talked vaguely about their businesses.

"What are they saying?" hissed Helen from the berth below. "Just idle chatter," I said.

I noticed from time to time, one or the other of the two men would leave the compartment. A moment later, the other would follow suit. They came back separately.

Helen was bemoaning her inability to understand Chinese, and I was trying to keep her quiet, convinced that we were being watched, and not wanting to reveal my facility with the language.

The talk between the two men wandered from business to their respective families, and eventually settled on the student movement.

Suddenly, the square-faced man stood up, and handed a pack of cigarettes to me with a smile. "Have a smoke?" he said.

"Thank you very much, I'd really enjoy one," I took the proffered cigarette. The man touched a match to it and I drew on it hungrily. It was the first smoke in three days. "You speak Chinese very well," smiled the square faced man. His eyes did not smile though. I had been tricked into revealing myself. "Thank you," I said trying to be nonchalant. The man sat down again and resumed his conversation with the fat man. I lay on the upper berth smoking and listening.

Presently the square-faced man turned to me and said, "What is your opinion of all this—teacher?" I was taken aback. "Do I look like a teacher?" I parried. The man laughed. "Aren't all foreigners in China teachers?" I laughed too. "What do you think of the student movement?" he persisted. I shrugged. "I'm a foreigner and it's none of my business." But he would not leave it. "But you must have some opinion." I resorted to the same answer I had given my students weeks before, using the allegory of the guest arriving at a friend's home and finding him quarrelling with his parent. "That is exactly my position," I said, and turning the question around asked, "How would you handle that situation?" He smiled and handed me another cigarette. I lit it with the butt of the first one.

22 May 1989   I was wakened by a light shining in my face. The train had pulled into a station. My companions in the compartment were all asleep. I put on my glasses and lifted a corner of the curtain. The station was called Jining. There was a soldier standing at attention every five or six feet along the platform. They did not seem to be armed. Each carried a flashlight a foot long. Passengers in neat queues trickled onto the train in complete silence. Suddenly all the lights on the platform went out. The soldiers' flashlights came on almost simultaneously, pointed to the ground. All that could be seen were the shiny tips of boots, and visors. I heard train doors shut, and footsteps moving quickly down the corridor.

The train began to move. I dropped the curtain and prepared to go back to sleep when it occurred to me that we were moving in the wrong direction. The train was slowly backing out of the station. My companions slept on.

The train slowed and stopped. I lifted the curtain again. It was pitch dark. When my eyes adjusted to the darkness, I saw that we had stopped beneath a high embankment. Soldiers carrying the same long flashlights lined the tracks. As soon as the train stopped they scrambled aboard. Booted footsteps ran down the corridor. I heard the woman conductor being told to lock the doors at both ends of the train, and the rattle of keys. There was silence for a while. My companions breathed softly and evenly in their sleep. However, the man with the square face who lay on his back, slept with his eyes open. I lay still wondering how long the man had been watching me. I had done nothing, I reasoned with myself. I had merely looked out the window. Maybe I saw things I was not supposed to.

After a time, I heard a lock grate, and the boots came down the corridor again. Our compartment was at the far end, but I could hear compartment doors being opened and banged shut. The boots came closer. They were outside the door. I pretended to sleep.

The door handle turned. "Foreigners," I heard the conductor whisper. "All?" I could not hear the conductor's reply, but the door did not open. "You can unlock now," a voice said, and the boots moved on. I dozed off. At dawn when I was wakened by the bright and cheery "good morning" broadcast that came over the P.A. system, the train had not moved. The fat man rolled off the upper berth and waddled out of the compartment. The man with the square face looked out the window, feigned surprise and went off to investigate. Helen slowly regained consciousness, and asked where we were and how long we'd been there. "Not long," I said. There was no point telling her we'd been waiting for six hours.

The fat man came back blinking and hissing through his newly brushed teeth. The other followed a little while later. "Has the train broken down?" I asked innocently. The square faced man gave me a searching look. "There were students on board," he said, "and the authorities want them off." "How many?" "Five." The fat man suddenly chimed in, "And we've been here six hours just for five students!" "They've found them," said the man with the square face, lighting a cigarette. "They're in the dining car."

All this while Helen was hissing, "What are they saying?" and I was trying to keep her quiet, feeding her tidbits of information.

The P.A. system crackled to life. "Good morning, dear passengers," a cheery female voice chirped. "Did you sleep well? Of course you did. Now you must be ready for breakfast. Our chefs have prepared a marvelous menu this morning." There followed the menu.

I slid off the upper berth, saying I was off to breakfast.

The conductor stood with her arms folded across her chest outside the dining car door. "No foreigners," she said shortly.

Over her shoulder, I could see five young men in a corner booth, surrounded by soldiers, deep in conversation.

"I want some breakfast," I said. "No foreigners in the dining car," the conductor replied grimly. She had been friendly and smiling when we boarded yesterday. But that was before the soldiers . . .

"Did you see?" Helen started as soon as I opened the compartment door. The two men were gone. I shut the door quickly and told her what I had seen. "For God's sake be still. We don't know who these two might be," I warned her.

Helen nodded like a small child.

Another two hours went by.

Suddenly the train doors were locked again. Soldiers armed with wooden clubs ran past the window toward the dining car. The fat man looked at his watch, got up and left. The man with the square face lit a fresh cigarette. "We'll be leaving soon," he said matter-of-factly.

In another half hour we were on our way. The fat man announced, "They've been taken off," as he sank into his seat. There was no sign of soldiers or students along the tracks. Perhaps the embankment hid them from view.

The train got progressively later. Time and again, we were shunted onto sidings to wait while long trains with blinds drawn sped by. There was no drinking water, and food was running out.

By the time we crawled into Beijing, we had been on the train twenty-eight hours.

It was dusk, and there was talk of curfew, but no one knew when it would begin. I put Helen in a taxi, and went in search of transportation for myself. After much haggling I finally convinced a cab-driver to take me to the institute for FEC.

"It's not that I'm greedy," the driver apologized, "but I haven't done any business in a week. There aren't any tourists, the business people have other arrangements."

The absence of foreigners has become noticeable.

The east end of Changan Street was blocked by two buses and a truck. The street dividers had been torn up and heaped on the barricade. We squeezed past the barricades, the driver cursing under his breath.

"To tell the truth, I'd sooner not be taking you," he said over his shoulder, because they've been commandeering taxis." "Who has?" "The students," he replied. "There's a wooden stick under your feet with a white cloth tied to it. Stick it through the window, or we might never get to the institute."

The road merged into the narrow eastbound street. Traffic moved in a steady stream. Little knots of people gathered along the way. Several taxis were stopped along the side, but our white flag worked its magic. Nearer the institute, students spilled onto the road from both sides. We slowed to a crawl, but we still weren't stopped. Students peered at me through the gathering gloom and flashed the V-for-Victory sign, which I returned.

We were stopped finally by a barricade. The driver apologized but the institute was in view. I gave him the FEC and got off. There was no traffic on the road at all. Students were everywhere.

"Blood Shed at Six Mile Bridge" screamed a new poster on a campus bulletin board. A silent crowd clustered around reading. G— came out of the crowd and grasped my arm.

"Where have you been?" he demanded, looking at the backpack. My trek to the Square the previous week had obviously gone the rounds. "I spent the weekend in Inner Mongolia," I said, feeling almost guilty. G—'s glance was disdainful. He took me by the arm and steered me away.

"While you were enjoying yourself, the police were beating us," he said bitterly. We walked across the darkened garden toward my apartment . G— spoke haltingly at first, not quite sure whether he could trust me. Then he became caught up in his own story and caution was thrown to the wind.

The previous morning, motorcyclists brought word that the army was moving into the city from the south at Six Mile Bridge. Their mission was to clear the Square. A— and the others who were on hunger strike, raced to Six Mile Bridge as fast as they could. The students formed a human barrier sitting across the roadway.

"A— was right in front, and I was next to him," said G— . "We sat and waited. The farmers in the neighborhood came out to watch. A few joined us. Others brought us food, and cigarettes. The riot police came in several lorries, armed with clubs and electric prods and teargas. We didn't move. This was a nonviolent protest. We would not respond to abuse, and we would not strike back. The police got off the lorries and charged us with clubs and prods."

A— was severely beaten, and so were several girls. But G— managed to come away unscathed. The farmers who had sympathized with the students all along came to their aid. The police were driven back with bricks and bottles and fence posts. The army was stopped. A— and a number of others were in hospital but G— either did not know or would not tell me which one.

The whole miserable thing was engulfing me again.

I took a long hot shower, had something to eat and dialed Helen. The phone was out of order again. It was after ten and there was no one to complain to till the morning. I tried to read but the words meant nothing.

There was an odd buzzing somewhere in the apartment, like a blue-bottle fly caught in a jar. I turned on the overhead light and looked about. The sound came from my desk, or near it. It was the phone. I quietly picked up the receiver. Right away a strange man's voice said, "Someone just picked up the phone." Silence. "Hello . . . Hello . . . " I could hear my voice rising. "Who is this?" asked the man on the other end. "You know who it is. I want to use this phone. Connect me!" "Hang up! Hang up!" shouted the man at the other end. The phone went dead. A moment later the buzzing started again. I picked up the receiver. A different voice said, "Are you 269?" "No." "Who are you?" "You know who I am. Connect my phone, please. Right now." I slammed down the receiver. I was shaking. For a long time we have been speculating on the probability that the Foreign Expert apartments may be bugged. What games were being played on my telephone? Who is 269? How much of my conversation has been heard? I picked up the receiver again. The phone was working. I am keeping the phone in my desk drawer from now on. Am I paranoid?

3

▶

28 May 1989   It is unusually hot. The heat and the quietness are getting on my nerves.

The Square simmers under the broiling sun. The buses,
the ambulances, and the Red Cross tents have vanished. The
hunger strike is over but the silent vigil continues. The
numbers on the Square were falling. Many of the strikers
have gone home. However, more arrive from other cities
every day, and once more the throng on the Square is
swelling.

I bought a watermelon and a bottle of white wine, a notch
or two better than the really cheap stuff to go with dinner.
J— arrived voraciously hungry, hollow eyed and badly in
need of a shower and a shave. I knew, without being told,
where he had been. We cooked a whole package of spaghetti
and he ate most of it. The conversation was rambling.
Although the Square was on both our minds, we were both
making conscious efforts to avoid it. After the meal, J—
made coffee and poured the brandy. Then we settled down
to a game of Chinese chess. This has become a ritual.

J— now claims I lose because I'm not aggressive enough.

"You have to hit first and you have to hit hard," he
slammed a chess piece down so hard it broke. The peculiar
glint in his eye told me he wasn't thinking about chess at all.
We made the next few moves in silence.

Then he told me about the statue.

"It's called the Goddess of Democracy," he said. "We
made it and we're putting it in the Square tomorrow."

The statue was hastily put together. There was no time to make an original, so students of the Art Academy used an existing statue of a man holding a torch as a base. The head was removed and replaced with that of a woman. The man's laborer's costume was transformed into a flowing robe.

I was dismayed by this new development.

"I thought the movement was over?" I said.

J— made a face and shook his head. He lit two cigarettes and handed me one. The question hovered over our heads.

Finally J— said, "The students are disagreeing among themselves."

The Bei Da faction under Wang Dan feel they have gone as far as they can and are for pulling out and going underground. The other faction from Qing Hua are more militant. They are for staying on the Square till 20 June when the People's Congress convenes, and they've called for volunteers from the provinces.

"And the statue is their symbol. A— has thrown in his lot with the militants!"

"And you?" I wanted to bite my tongue off the moment I asked.

J— flashed me his open, little boy's smile. My heart sank.

We made a few more desultory moves and the game was over. I lost.

30 May 1989   "It is u-g-l-y !" cried Marc in his nasally New York accent. We were seated around the dinner table in the dining hall. Since Bill stopped eating in the dining hall, Marc has taken his place as the expert of experts. Now he is an expert on the aesthetics of modern Chinese art. The statue, he declared, is a cheap copy of the one in New York harbor.

"And they couldn't even get it right!" He complained she had no book; and where is her crown?

A group of us had gone to see the statue this afternoon. It had to be moved to the Square in three sections. Because the police had got wind of this, and were ordered to stop it from being erected, the pieces had to be carried by flat-decked tricycles through the back alleys and lanes of Beijing.

The Goddess is ten meters tall, made of plaster of Paris over a wooden frame. She is dressed in a shapeless robe that could be caftan, toga, or kimono. Her arms are extended forward, slightly crooked at the elbows, and a flaming torch is grasped in both hands. Her head is thrown back, face tilted upward. Her shoulder-length hair streams in the wind. She is quite beautiful. I was told she was modeled after a Chinese pop singer. I thought she looked "foreign." Her features were far too Caucasian. Although there was nothing even vaguely threatening about the statue, it made me quiver inside.

The statue became a rallying point and the Square has suddenly filled up again. Although most of the banners were from schools outside Beijing, there were a few local ones too. Our students were there as long as A— was. The faraway look of the poet-thinker which I noticed when he was on hunger strike, had darkened and intensified after the vicious beating he received at Six Mile Bridge. With his quiet, feline grace and his burning eyes, A— was a natural leader.

The clubs and the cattle-prods at Six Mile Bridge were only a warning of things to come. Although the state still called the movement a patriotic demonstration, it was also hinting more often that "a small number of people" were bent on "disrupting society" and "outside intervention" and meddling in China's internal affairs. These are far more sophisticated terror tactics than one realizes. By not pointing the finger in any one direction it leaves the populace to ponder where that moving finger might finally come to rest. The effect is to have everyone looking over his or her shoulder. The statue was a tangible on which the state could hang its case and say, "See, it is a foreign conspiracy!"

These days it is impossible to sit at table without hearing about the Goddess. The Germans, with their love of symbols, were elated. The French students took "La Liberté" to their sentimental hearts. The Americans saw this as further proof that democracy is alive and well in China, except the Southern Baptists and the Mormons, who think they have brought this about through their clamoring to God. The Russians take reams of photographs and say nothing. The Japanese are concerned only about their business ventures in China. What happens to the people is immaterial.

Edward disappears into the city every morning by bus or on his bicycle and does not return till dark. He says he has been studying the works of Mateo Ricci kept in a small museum near the tomb of the great Jesuit in the center of the city. But I don't believe him. There is a nervous intensity about him that worries me. There are too many sides to this ascetic young man. The worst of it is that there is no one he can talk to.

The movement has taken on horrific proportions for the Howards. They are a nice academic couple who have spent their lives in a small Midwestern town. Academe is comfortable, middle-class, white, and Christian. China was their first trip off the American continent, and for them it was tantamount to stepping off the edge of the earth. They are here for only one semester, and for the first bit lived precariously in their cocoon. That fragile shell has cracked. The realities of life are dreadful to confront at any age. But the experience is especially poignant for the middle-aged for whom life has always been as calm as a duck pond.

This evening, Dorothy Howard and I went looking for L—, one of her freshman students. L— had been beaten at Six Mile Bridge. We had no idea where his dormitory was in the four-story building. But we needn't have worried. Each grade occupies one floor, and the freshmen are at the top.

L— is small and skinny. He looks about fourteen, though he is probably twenty. He had been beaten about the head and shoulders and repeatedly kicked in the groin. He lay like a limp rag doll on his bunk, barely able to open his eyes, for the light aggravated his headache. He tried valiantly to sit up, to talk, but the effort was too great. In the end we just sat. Dorothy held the boy's slim, white hand in hers, and I could see her jaw line tighten with anguish. She is a genuinely kindhearted woman.

L— smiled almost happily. He was visited by two foreign teachers, who had brought canned meats and fruit. He had gained much "face" in the eyes of his peers who clustered about him. L— had been hospitalized together with A—. The two had signed themselves out and half crawled, half carried each other back to campus.

"A— has gone back to the Square," L— whispered through parched lips. "I should be there too." "No. You stay in bed," I said sternly. The boy smiled and nodded. "A— says you are a tough taskmaster," he whispered. The others giggled. I left my phone number with one of the girls and told her to call me if L— needed anything. I did not like the persistent headaches, the poor coordination, and the fever. As we came down the stairs, Dorothy took my arm, her face crumbling. We came back here and I poured us a couple of stiff Scotches.

30 May 1989   Joe's bar is a funny little place on the north road. Heaven knows what it's real name is, but it's Joe's to foreigners of five institutions. At night the doorway is lit by pink neon tubes. Beyond the beaded curtain that covers the entrance there is a tiny bar. Joe is a young man with a handlebar moustache and shoulder-length hair who tends bar and cooks the few items of food on the menu. On the shelf under the bar mirror is an impressive array of bottles, mostly imported. There are six narrow booths lining the walls of the room beyond plus a couple of tiny round tables in the center. Julio Iglesias is crooning. . . *For all the girls I've loved before . . .* on the stereo. Colored lights flickering according to the cadence of the music turn our faces into grotesque masks crisscrossed by many colors.

The Howards, Judy, a soft-spoken young woman from the deep south, and I are getting quietly sloshed. My chest is hurting and I cannot seem to find a comfortable angle at which to sit. I ache. It is the beer, of course, and there is half a bottle left. The others are slurring words and giggling. There is two of me now. One that aches and wants to stop drinking, and the other devil-may-care one won't stop. I hunch my shoulders and lean forward. That eases the pain so I freeze in that position. The others giggle. I must look very funny.

When we stumbled out of Joe's it was pitch dark. A few lorries lumbered by going east out of the city. There is hardly anything going toward the city. It's past curfew time. There aren't any soldiers around yet, but people are saying that they've been coming in by the busload disguised as tourists, and that the underground city is filled with them. I believe it. A variation of the Trojan horse trick. Nothing changes.

31 May 1989   There was a violent knock on the door after nine. It was a knock that I have grown used to without liking. J— was leaning on the jamb, grinning puckishly. "I brought someone to see you," he said, and A— stepped around him out of the shadows into the light. A— grabbed my hand and squeezed it. "That day—on the Square—and the food parcel you sent to the dorm," he stumbled, groping for words, and finally crumbled into laughter, "You're great." J— went into the kitchen to make coffee. I could hear him moving around in there making a great clatter, and singing under his breath, *"For all the girls I've loved before . . . "*

A— settled on the sofa. He was very pale and drawn. He moved almost cautiously as people in pain are wont to do. I asked if he was all right. He smiled.

"I was sitting on the ground when they charged me. They hit the girl first. I tried to push her out of the way." The first few blows of the electric cattle prod landed on his ribs. Then they went for his groin. "I thought I was dying," said A—. Then someone kicked him in the head and everything went black. He woke on a pallet in the corridor of an overcrowded hospital the next day.

"They wanted to keep me there, but I wanted to be here. So L— and I signed ourselves out."

The coffee was strong when it came. A— downed his in

a few gulps and asked for more.

"Actually he's very hungry," J— said. A— tried to smile but looked stricken.

"What about French toast?" said J—. "What about spaghetti?" I countered. "What is spaghetti?" asked A —, getting over his embarrassment. Once more J— was in the kitchen rattling pots and pans and singing, darting back and forth to join in the conversation. While A— ate, J— went over to the bookcase and took down the brandy and three glasses. "Shall I hit you again?" He picked that up from some movie he'd seen. "Why not," I tossed back at him. J— set down the brandy glasses. We each took one. "Here's to looking at you, kid." Bogart from *Casablanca*.

The food and brandy relaxed A—. J— found the tape of the "second son's" music and put it on. He sprawled on the sofa, blowing cigarette smoke at the ceiling, listening. For a while no one spoke. I smoked my pipe and sipped the brandy and the music wove around me like a warm blanket.

"That's great," A— sighed when the tape ended. "I want to play and sing like that some day, and have people listen." "But you do play and sing. And people listen," I said. "I've listened." His brow knitted. I knew he was thinking, that's now. But soon he will be out in the real world with no control over his future. A sobering thought.

He suddenly laughed, and it was like the sun shining through the clouds.

"When they hit me down there, I thought I was finished as a man," he said. "But there's a girl now, and she . . ." he faltered, and looked stricken again. "Helped?" I said, grabbing words out of the air. A— brightened. "It's okay," he said.

"We call this the three R's movement," said J—. "It stands for rock and roll and romance."

The ghetto-blasters have been going day and night in the dormitories lately. Boys and girls are in each other's dormitories all the time. It is as though they were shutting out the ugliness of the world around them with sensation and passion; holding tomorrow at bay behind a wall of sound.

Before they left, I voiced my uneasiness about the way

the movement was going and begged them not to go back to the Square.

‹ "I'm not going back," said J—. "I have to take care of myself and be a great writer." "And I won't go back," echoed A—. "I'm in love." I shut the door behind them. I could hear J— softly singing, *"For all the girls I loved before . . ."* all the way down the long corridor.

2 June 1989   Pieter, my German colleague from last year, gave a dinner party at his place for a group of young Chinese artists. Pieter is a collector of Chinese bric-a-brac, and we spent the afternoon driving across the city in his green Toyota to examine a small Ming bowl at Liulichang. It was crudely made, lopsided, and did not have the government's red stamp, designating it as a historic artifact cleared for export. I wouldn't have it if it were given to me. Pieter chewed his moustache, unable to make up his mind. We went to several other shops. Pieter hunched his shoulders and shook his head. I know him well enough to read the signs. He was determined to buy something; anything.

Suddenly, he turned to me with an astonished look on his face. "It's four o'clock," he almost shouted. "So?" "The guests will be coming soon, and we are not ready." "We?" "You are coming. That goes without saying!" His long legs were rapidly devouring the distance to his car. That's how I happened to be at this party.

I had gone to visit Pieter at the Friendship Hotel in the afternoon, intending to stay for the "depressing movie of the week"—Chinese films are usually awash with tears—and return on the Friday night school bus. The scheduled film was a black comedy. *The Trouble Shooters* contained nudity, sex and violence, and had been pulled off the public screens. But it was considered acceptable for foreigners, who were hardened to such evils. However, at seven o'clock I was answering the door and pouring drinks. Marvelous aromas wafted from the kitchen where Pieter and his student, Eva, were concocting the meal.

The guest of honor was Wang Deren, a young man of twenty-six and already notorious for what he calls "art in motion." For example, last year he undertook a long and expensive journey to the foothills of the Himalayas where he taped two strips of tinsel in the shape of a cross at the foot of a knoll which the Buddhists revere. Eventually the wind destroyed the cross and scattered the pieces. That was one of his tamer works.

The escapade that brought the wrath of the gods down on Wang's head took place in March. There was an exhibition of modern art at the National Gallery. Wang ran along the gallery above the main entrance pelting the crowd below with two-thousand condoms stuffed with his name card. Whether his antics can be called art is a matter of opinion. (Personally, I consider it the wasteful but harmless self-indulgence of an egocentric.) Nevertheless, Wang was arrested, beaten and released. He was placed under house arrest and forbidden to practice any form of art for the rest of his life. Wang had escaped from the place he lived in, and moved from one safe-house to another. He was a fugitive.

I had heard of Wang Deren and his works from both J— and A— who moved in the murky half-world of bohemian artists. Young people seem taken with his independence and look upon him as a messianic figure in modern Chinese art. Indeed there is a certain resemblance to Christ in his narrow, pale, ascetic face framed by shoulder length hair and a short beard. The four young men who came with him, also artists, in their garish tie-dyed shirts, chains and bangles and rings and things seemed to have crawled out of '60s California. None of them spoke English or German, so I was again the interpreter. R. W. , who had recently married an English woman colleague of mine, made a fifth. His artistic outlook is more academic, and therefore more conventional. Moreover he is attached to the army. R. W. was out of place in this group. I was surprised that he had come without his new bride.

Pieter is an excellent cook. The wine flowed freely, and so did the conversation. R. W. retreated to a corner, looking glum.

At the end of the evening, he insisted on walking me to the bus. When we were alone he suddenly grasped my shoulder so hard that it made me flinch.

"Whatever you do, stay away from the Square this weekend," he whispered.

I nodded. He released my shoulder. We faced each other across a chasm that was not there before.

"Thank you for your friendship," he said, stretching out his hand. I clasped it in mine. R. W. always shakes hands warmly. This time he held on to my hand as though we might never see each other again. Yet we had arranged to meet for dinner Sunday night. I got onto the bus. R. W. stood and waited till we turned out of the parking lot. He did not wave.

4 June 1989

DEAR SONS,

I have never felt so desolate, and never more thankful that you are not here. There has been no mail service for a week, so I don't know when this will get posted. But what has been happening needs to be recorded.

They say the eye of the storm is dead calm. That's the way it has been the last fortnight. Dead calm. Heat and smog lay like a brown pall over the city. The throng on the Square had thinned. It was clear that the state would not respond to the students' demands. The waiting game had broken the back of the movement. Factional strife broke out. Wang Dan of Beijing University was all for ending the sit-in and taking the movement underground. But the more militant faction led by Wu'er Kaixi and Chai Ling would not give up the fight. Our students had come off the Square. Many have gone home. But students from other cities poured in by the trainloads and the sit-in continued.

Life seemed almost normal on campus though there were no classes. A few students crawled about listless and exhausted. However the relentless blare of ghetto-blasters was silent. A scant two weeks ago the mood was buoyant and hopeful. Now they seem to mark time, waiting for something to happen. The waiting is sapping us all.

The storm finally broke.

Hope died on the streets of Beijing, in the dark hours before dawn, mowed down by automatic weapons and tanks.

Ours is one of five institutions of higher learning strung between two major highways leading to the city center. All yesterday the noose tightened. A troop train arrived at a junction about twenty kilometers east of us early Saturday morning (3 June). Tough young men on motorcycles, the moneychangers of Retanlu,* rode hell bent for leather spreading the word from campus to campus. Once the alarm was given, students of five institutions rushed to raise barricades. Two buses and a truck were parked across the highway west of the campus gate. The local populace tore off doors, collected scrap metal and lumber, pushed down walls for bricks to use as missiles. Old ladies rolled rags for Molotov cocktails.

The commotion drew me out of my apartment. All morning I had waited for A— or J— but neither appeared. The dormitories were empty except for a few party members like Willie and G— who lay curled on their bunks plugged into their walkmans."A— has gone to the Square," said Willie cheekily. "He'll get his." He winked broadly. There are times I could wring the young scoundrel's neck. But it won't do to show any emotion. I left the room without a word.

I suspected A— and the others would be out there. In retrospect I think I also knew there was no way I could get them off. But I had to try. Traffic was reduced to a trickle on the south road. Students were directing the flow around the barricade. The public buses were stopped, but smaller vehicles and bicycles were getting through. I flagged a jitney. The ticket-taker recognized me and let me squeeze on. "Going into town?" "Shopping," I said. She looked at me gravely and let it go.

*Retan Street.

I got off at the train station at the end of the run. The station square was a sea of heads. There were many green uniforms. The riot police and the army wear uniforms so similar it is hard to tell which is which. There were many young people, taking advantage of the government's offer of free passage and going home. The green uniforms were checking identities. I pushed my way to Changan Street and turned east. The crowd thinned to almost normal except for the absence of buses.

The sun beat down on the Square. At the northeast corner near the Statue of the Goddess was the campsite of Beijing University and Qinghua University. Close by was a tent in which four celebrities, including the rock singer, Hou Dejian, were staging a seventy-two-hour hunger strike. I threaded my way through the jumble of campsites. The ground was slick with litter and garbage trampled to a sticky mush. Fetid fumes writhed in the hot, still air. I found A— and the others at the foot of the monument where they had been before. They were silent, seated cross-legged on the pavement. Leaning against each other, embracing, holding hands. A— was picking a melody on his guitar. A young girl sat with her back leaning against his, her head cradled in the hollow of his shoulder. None of them noticed me until I spoke. A— scrambled to his feet and essayed a smile.

"You promised," I started to say, and got no further.

A—'s face had changed. The smoothness of youth had been remoulded into the planes and angles of manhood. The eyes blazed with passion. The smile, when it came, was sad but serene. He drew the girl possessively to him, holding her in the crook of one arm.

"This is my lover," he said.

She smiled, her little pointed chin held high, until she realized there was no need for defiance with me. Quickly, I told A— what was happening, and begged him to withdraw while there was still time. He listened, his head bowed gravely until I finished. We looked at each other as across a great gulf. I thought I had made a good plea, but I failed.

A—'s eyes were unfathomable pools. "We've known they were coming since yesterday," he said. "Then why are you here?" I had to fight to keep my voice down. He looked at me almost pityingly. "Because some have to die." I swallowed the protest that rose ready to my lips. We had been over that ground before. "You must go. Quickly," he said. "There are eyes everywhere." I nodded. I had already been photographed several times in the last two weeks. "There is one thing you can do for us," said A— as I turned away. I nodded. He handed me a brown paper bag containing a bundle of envelopes neatly tied with a red hair band. "They're wills and last letters to parents and friends," he said. "Mail them for us." I nodded, blinking back tears. Only several evenings ago A— was talking confidently about the job he had lined up with a tourist hotel. He would stay in Beijing after graduation even if it meant enduring the hardships of being without a residence permit. At least he would be in the city where he could pursue his music. He wanted to try acting, and some day, directing. All that was gone.

There was nothing more to say. We embraced and wished each other good health. Some of the others came and shook hands. Many of them I didn't even know. The girl took my hand and guided me through the throng to the edge of the Square. A student from another college going east offered me a ride on the back of his bicycle for a distance. When he turned off Changan Street I thanked him and continued on foot. Beyond the Friendship Store the road was completely blocked off. I turned north and walked as far as Chauyang Road. The streets were swarming with people and traffic was snarled. I managed to jump on a bus heading east. It was supper time before I reached campus again.

In the meantime, a convoy was stopped outside the south gate of the campus since the afternoon. Students and locals swarmed over the tank at the head of the column, and the trucks and armored personnel carriers full of soldiers that followed. The soldiers were armed, bewildered but friendly. Most were young farm boys, no more than eighteen or nineteen.

I mingled with the crowd listening to the banter between students and soldiers. The soldiers had been kept in isolation since April, and seemed ignorant as to why they were being moved into the capital. Some thought it was an exercise; others thought they were making a film (the army has its own film unit); a few said there might have been "trouble" in the city. Many asked the meaning of the two-fingered V-for-Victory sign that the students used, and promptly adopted it themselves. The stalemate lasted all day. Students and locals brought cigarettes, beer and food to the soldiers. They chatted and laughed. It was friendly till after dark.

Suddenly, the lead tank started up and rammed through the barricade, slicing the buses into halves and setting them ablaze. The truck behind roared after it. A student hanging onto the door of the cab was shot at point-blank range. His friends who caught him as he fell, were peppered with machine gun fire. The crowd responded with a hail of bricks and Molotov cocktails. The canvas canopy over a truck caught fire. It jackknifed into a ditch and exploded with the young soldiers trapped under it.

Suddenly I saw G—, a wispy youth who wouldn't hurt a fly, sprinting toward a jeep carrying three officers. I tried to stop him but he knocked me out of his way, and heaved a brick into the driver's face. The jeep careened into a tree. G— leaped on the driver, wielding a fence post. The crowd dragged the officers into the fields. I lost G— in the confusion. Bricks and bottles were flying in every direction, mingled with intermittent bursts of gunfire. I ducked behind a low wall, and keeping to the shadows, sprinted for the campus gate. The crowd fell back and dispersed. The convoy broke loose and raced toward the Square.

A silent line formed outside the school clinic. Inside, a nurse and doctor with stony faces washed and dressed wounds. We were lucky. No one was shot.

Armed with a half bottle of Chinese brandy from which I had fortified myself, I went looking for G—. I found him cowering in a corner of his dorm, covered with blood.

He babbled incoherently between chattering teeth while I helped him peel off his bloody clothes. Some of his dorm mates fetched water in a basin and between us washed the blood off his face, arms and hands. There was a lot of blood, but he was not hurt. I poured enough brandy into G— to stop a horse. G— was like a frightened child. "Don't go away," he pleaded, hanging onto my wrist. "I'll stay," I said. Finally he slept, his fingers gasped so tightly around my wrist I had to pry them apart. I bundled up his clothes and dumped them in a garbage container at the far end of campus. G— who loved poetry, and wondered at the intricacies of a peony, will never be the same.

For some unknown reason during the evening a spotlight was hastily rigged to light up the back of the building where I live. There were men lurking in the shadows watching. I, who hate drawing curtains even at home, drew them. Though I could not see them, I could hear them speaking in a dialect I do not understand. I tried to sleep, but the light was in my eyes, and with the blinds drawn the heat was unbearable.

All night the convoy rumbled on. The sound had become a continuous and distant roar. I could no longer tell whether it was going toward the city or away from it. Shooting started again before dawn. The spotlight was shot out. The darkness was terrifying. A disembodied voice howled, "They're killing people!"

I lay between sleeping and waking, dimly wondering, "Should I get my passport? My money? Call the embassy? Get out of bed?" When my brain cleared I told myself there was nothing I could do. A bullet destined for me will find me. So I lay quite still, frightened but calm. After a while the roar of the convoy and the rattle of gunfire ceased. An oppressive silence crashed down upon me. Every nerve in my body was alive and screaming. I shut my eyes and forced myself to stay still. As the sky lightened I dozed.

Part Four

▶

After the Storm

4 June 1989   The day dawned dark and gloomy. Black clouds blanket the city. The air is heavy, humid and hot, threatening rain that does not come. Thunder—or is it artillery fire—rumbles to the east. There is a complete news blackout. One cryptic phrase is repeated over the radio and on TV: "Tiananmen Square has been cleared." Rumors were flying. B—, the young man on the front desk whom none of us likes or trusts, was on duty and really quite full of himself.

I avoid talking to the man, but he seems to know things. "Any news of our students?" He grinned, showing all his fangs, naming two professors who were combing the city hospitals and morgues for students. "Accurate information is hard to get," his head tilted speculatively to one side. "We'll have to wait . . . and hope for the best." I walked past him into the empty dining hall. The others are keeping to their apartments.

Eyewitness accounts of the horror went up on the bulletin boards in the afternoon. Faculty and a few students clustered around reading. A wall of silence and fear has gone up overnight. People avoid each other. Faculty friends ducked and ran when they saw me. Students stared and smiled sheepishly, not knowing whether to leave or stay and talk.

Marc, looking bedraggled, stressed, and more obnoxious than before he turned forty, lamented that he would have gone out there and gotten some great shots had he known in

171

time. I almost hit him. As it was I went up one side and down the other and gave him what was no doubt the tongue-lashing of his life.

By late afternoon the survivors began to trickle back to campus. A list of the missing that was posted went on and on. Half my class was on it. I could not bear to read it all.

About four in the afternoon J— came to see me. His hair had been cropped so short he was practically bald. One lens of his glasses was cracked. His clothes obviously did not belong to him. He brought a young girl with him who was from another institute in the neighborhood.

"This is my lover," said J—, introducing us.

The girl, terribly young and shy, hung her head and blushed. The world and all its turmoil had caught her unprepared; seized her in its maw and shook her to the deepest fibers of her being. Yet under the vulnerability I perceived an indomitable spirit. I warmed to her at once. Within a very short time she will need that wellspring of strength.

I shoved the phone into my desk drawer, for I'm convinced it's bugged, put on some Wagner and turned up the volume. Still, we talked in whispers. J— was manning the barricades outside the institute and missed going to the Square.

"She prevented me from going," J— said. The girl's eyes brimmed but her chin came up proudly.

There had been a pitched battle when the convoy broke through the barricade. J— attacked an officer. I knew he was going underground and we would not see each other again for a long time. Ironically, I had a huge sum of money in my desk, having just received some royalties from a book. J— is fiercely proud. His family is not poor. But mail has not been getting through to the students for weeks, and I guessed he was out of funds. I pressed a few hundred on him.

A— was on the Square and had not returned. "He'll show up," J— reassured me.

J— had not eaten since the previous day. Neither had the girl. We cooked all the food I had: half a pound of dumplings, vegetables, eggs, and a can of chicken. We toasted each other with the last of the Glenffiddich. It was fitting. We exchanged addresses and photographs. J— gripped me by the shoulders, eyes shining. "Dad," he said, "I've always wanted to call you—Dad." I tried to smile but my face felt stiff. "Son," I barely managed. The three of us embraced, and they left.

All that evening and into the next day snatches of "The Funeral March" sounded over the PA system. Every time it did some mysterious hand struck out a name from the list of the missing on the bulletin board. From time to time a name would be bawled over the PA, in a voice inhuman with grief, "Where are you?" And the echoes would bounce around the quadrangle, ghostly, disembodied, horrible to hear.

There were survivors. One young girl who had been beaten over the head was mute. I found her cowering in a corner of her dormitory like a frightened animal. I took her food. She was afraid at first, shrinking into a corner as if she would push herself into the wall. Her mouth gaped in horrible silent screams. I spoke to her quietly, reassuring her with my voice. All at once the fight went out of her. She clung to me like a child. I coaxed some noodles into her. She ate automatically. When she was calmer she scribbled disjointed notes from which I pieced together her story. She was camped with the rest of our students at the foot of the monument and had been among those that were permitted to evacuate from the southeast end of the Square. A corridor wide enough for only one person to pass at a time was opened, lined on both sides by soldiers. The soldiers struck at them with cattle prods and knives as they passed. She had been hit over the head and at the back of the neck.

Another girl, D—, was also on the Square at the institute's campsite at the foot of the monument. When the shooting started at the north end of the Square they remained where they were.

D— is a quiet girl who is very bright but never said much in class. Now she babbled. The words tumbled out as fast as she could form them.

"Some of my classmates had joined the long line leaving through the exit at the south of the Square. We could hear the tanks, the shots and the screaming. People were running and falling all around us."

D— was buried under the pile of her companions.

M—, a young man whom I taught, was near the statue when the tanks arrived. Hou Dejian, the fasting rock star, negotiated with the commandant to allow the students to leave peacefully from the south end of the Square. The order to that effect was broadcast across the Square. He could see movement in the distance as the crowd slowly dispersed. The students at the north end of the Square remained seated on the ground. Suddenly the light went out. The Square was plunged into darkness. Search lights came on. The tanks began to roll. M— said he watched in horror as the students lay down in their path, hands linked.

"They were singing 'The Internationale' when the tanks rolled over them. Then they started shooting."*

Somehow he made his way back to their campsite. He said he dragged D— from the crush of people who were crowding out of the square. Together they crawled to the edge of the Square and hid behind a row of garbage containers.

They lost track of time. Finally the shooting stopped. There were screams and moans everywhere. He claimed they watched the soldiers bulldoze the fallen, dead and alive, into heaps, pour gasoline on them and set them aflame. Huge flames shot up, and the Square filled with acrid black smoke.

M— sobbed hysterically as he told his story. "Some were alive!" he kept saying over and over.

M— and D— laid low until the Square quieted and the soldiers were busy cleaning up. Then they slipped down an alley. They managed to put some distance between themselves and the Square, keeping to the alleys and lanes heading east. The institute seemed to be the only haven.

---

*The most reliable reports of events at Tiananmen Square, however, indicate that the soldiers did not fire directly at students, but overhead. The actual "massacre" took place in streets some distance from Tiananmen. —ED.

Soldiers patrolled the main roads, shooting at random. As they came to the end of an alley they ran into a patrol. M— was shot in the leg. They played dead until the soldiers left. Fortunately, it was a flesh wound. The girl half carried and half dragged him to Chungwenmen Hospital, where he was treated.

While the doctor was still bandaging the wound, a patrol arrived demanding to search the wards. A nurse who tried to prevent them was shot on the spot. The doctor hid them in the morgue while the soldiers searched. Later, he smuggled them to his quarters through a back door. They stayed in the doctor's rooms until it was daylight. It took them more than ten hours to get back. M— and D— have also gone underground.

L— stood leaning against the door jamb of his dormitory. The building was practically empty. He had a bulging backpack at his feet. All his personal treasures, the posters of racing cars, American film stars, and the New York skyline had gone from the walls. He stood there shaking like a leaf. He came towards me when he saw me holding onto the wall. One leg dragged.

"I'm going home, teacher," he tried to smile, but didn't quite make it. "Where is home?" I tried to sound conversational, as I studied him. L— had not recovered from the beating two weeks earlier. He named a city eighteen hours away by train. "Are you going alone?" "There are others from there. We will go together." "Where are they?" He gulped awkwardly, and bowed his head. "Money?" I asked. He nodded, dumb with misery.

I have never been so glad at having money. It was time to spend it.

Presently, the others returned. They had stolen some bicycles. H—, a tall strapping Mongolian, who was older and stronger than the others would take L— on his handlebars.

I handed a wad of bills to H— which he stuffed into his jeans.

"This will get us home," he said. The others had gone out to the bicycles which could not be left unattended. He offered me a cigarette and we smoked in the empty dormitory. H— sat hunched over, his head in his hands.

"Were you there?" I asked. He looked up at me with his black opaque eyes, and his head dropped again. We did not exchange another word till the cigarettes were finished.

H— got to his feet, and looked about the room almost regretfully, and he sighed. It was not easy for a Mongolian sheep-herder's son to get to university. "Do your sons go on strike?" he asked with his back to me, but I could hear the tears in his voice. "Not like this," I said. "Why?" "Because they have no reason to." He turned to me, and his narrow, upward slanting eyes spat fire. "Do you understand what has been happening?" "I try to," I answered. He paced rapidly up and down the room, arms flailing the air. "We don't want to overthrow the regime. Communism has done a lot for this country, and we have no alternative. All we want is some improvements; some control over our own lives, so that we can fulfill our potential and the country's." The outburst seemed to exhaust him. He leaned his head against a bunk, breathing hard. I wanted to reach out to him, but I could not move. He turned and fixed me with his eyes. "Someone must tell the outside. You." H—'s six-foot frame loomed over me. I nodded. He sighed. The tension went out of him and he sagged. We smoked another cigarette, turned out the light and locked the door. The building was deserted. Our footsteps echoed all the way up and down the stairwell. I walked them to the gate. The road was pitch dark. They rode without lights. With luck they would make it to Tianjin, 123 miles away, and from there jump a train.

I stumbled back to my apartment blind with fatigue. There was a note under my door.

"A few of us are having a drink and some food in my apartment. Do come. Veronica."

Dear Veronica, the Earth Mother who was always looking out for the rest of us.

There were the Howards and Judy, Veronica and I. I picked at some cold lasagna and tossed off some beer. We tried to talk, but none of us could sustain a conversation.

The Howards were the first to voice what was on all our minds: it's time to go home.

5 June 1989   All morning, I could hear the rumbling of tanks and APCs grinding along the road. Now and then there was a burst of gunfire. A few stray bullets had hit the wall on the upper floors. But no one was hurt. I burrowed into my work. It was the only way I could keep my mind from racing around like a squirrel in a cage.

The embassy had sent me a form letter a week or ten days earlier, which I read and stuffed into a drawer. It offered advice on dealing with the crisis situation: "Avoid crowds—do not travel—stock up on canned goods—fill the bathtub with water in case the supply is cut off." It seemed so trite and silly at the time that I dismissed it out of hand. But I remembered an emergency number on it and decided it was time to try it.

I was a long time getting through. The sergeant major who finally came on the line was polite but vague. It took him awhile to comprehend that he was speaking to a fellow Canadian and another while to figure out where I am. "Well, sir," he said after some deliberation, during which he probably referred to a map, "we don't think you're in danger." "What should I do?" "Stay where you are," he said using a voice one would use on a fretful child. I hung up.

There was an uproar in the dining hall at lunch. The Germans were being evacuated. They were already bringing down their baggage, and an embassy car was on its way. As soon as I sat down Dick came over and sat down. "What have you heard?" he stuttered. "Nothing much," I said, doggedly shoveling rice into my mouth. "The Germans are being evacuated to the Great Wall Hotel where it will be safer, until they get flown out. We're thinking of going with them. What about you? There's room in the car." I thought about it and dismissed the idea at once. The embassy knows I am here. Besides I couldn't just pick up and leave. I decided to tell Dick about my conversation with the embassy. After all he is also Canadian.

Dick fidgeted nervously with his fly as each new idea clicked through his mind. "You must phone them again," he said. "When I've finished eating." "But the Germans will be gone—and— " "Go with them if you want. I just feel it's better for me to stay right here." He let that sink in, and sat fidgeting until I'd finished. "Now you must phone," he said and hustled me through the door.

Once more, I got the sergeant major on the line. I told him the Germans were being evacuated and asked whether he had any new advice to give. He did not think the Great Wall Hotel was safer than campus. "However, you are perfectly welcome to come to the embassy," he concluded. "You won't be very comfortable. We're quite crowded and you'll probably have to sleep on the floor." There followed a discussion of transportation. The embassy could not pick us up. We would have to make our own way there. I said I would think about it, thanked him and hung up.

Dick was crestfallen when I told him what the sergeant major had to say. "I don't think Maisy is going to like sleeping on the floor," he said. "This is an emergency, not some god damn picnic," I exploded. Dick's eyes went wide with astonishment. "I think I better ask Maisy," he stuttered, tugging at his zipper as he went out the door.

There were few people at dinner. Dick and Maisy did not leave. They were lamenting that the trip home on the Trans-Siberian Railway which they planned for July was out of the question now. "But we must have a holiday in Asia before going home," Maisy said in her nasal whine. So for an hour we talked about the pros and cons of Bali versus Thailand. It was trivia, but it got my mind off the realities.

6 June 1989   The Russian and American students were pulled out of campus today. The Russians were a volatile bunch, brimming with energy and good humor. I never really got to know them. There was a great deal of hugging and back-thumping and tears. The sad part is that friendships end right there. No addresses were exchanged. No "drop-me-a-postcard-sometime." This episode in their lives is over. *C'est la vie.*

The two young Southern Baptists went clutching their

bibles openly now, steadfast in their self-righteousness. Wally, the Mormon remains. The Howards are leaving tomorrow. I am glad. This whole experience is getting too much to bear. Besides they have other problems at home.

I was at the Howards, bidding them farewell, when the door burst open and Marc tumbled in six sheets to the wind, raging incoherently that the Baptists had betrayed him.

"They left without me!" he screeched. "The school's not doing anything to get me out! I'll die here! Bastards! They skipped out on me!" He sank into a chair, buried his head in his hands and cried. We looked on stunned and helpless. It was Dorothy who broke the silence, put her arms around him and tried to comfort him. Marc was frightened out of his mind. All his bravado was gone. All that was left was naked panic.

"I'm getting out of here," he gulped. "I'm going to the Great Wall, and I'll get the first flight there is—and I'm out of this god damn country!"

It was not clear whether the institute was providing a car or he was getting a cab, but transportation was on the way. He hugged the Howards, and extended a clammy hand to me. I felt indescribably sad. We had been friends. Now in this moment of crisis we were strangers. "If you ever come to New York, we'll have a drink, okay?" "Yes of course." He went quickly from the room.

N— phoned sounding tired and depressed. The familiar laughing gurgle in her voice was missing. I could hear the rattle of gunfire in the background. The army was still shooting in the streets south of the Square. An old woman eating lunch in an apartment above N—'s was killed by a stray bullet.

A student, X—, who lives in the western suburbs, was more graphic when he called. His rumor was that two opposing factions of the army were fighting for control of a military airfield west of the city. Artillery was being used. This would confirm the rumbling we heard from time to time over the last few days. He could not tell which unit was fighting which. In between gun battles, the local populace went out and chatted with the soldiers. X— said there were a lot of deserters roaming the streets, some of them armed.

The city is in chaos. None of the national leaders have appeared. The army is devouring itself like a wounded snake. This could escalate into civil war. For the first time since the movement began, I feel personally threatened. I call the emergency number of the embassy again. This time a Chinese voice answers. I demand to speak to a Canadian. There is some waffling, but a Canadian voice comes on the line. Once more I go through the rigamarole of who I am, where I am and so on.

"There is an evacuation flight tomorrow morning," he tells me, "but I don't know if you'll get on. It's strictly first come, first served. Do you want me to put you on the list?" Of course I do. "You'll have to be at the embassy tonight, sir. The flight leaves early in the morning." I ask whether the embassy could send a car, as there are three Canadians on campus. The man on the line was polite but quite adamant that the embassy car was otherwise engaged. I explained that the institute would be willing to provide transportation, but it would not be safe, particularly since it was after 4:00 P.M. and curfew was on. However, an embassy car flying an embassy flag would get through unmolested.

In the ensuing silence, I could hear the gears in the man's civil service mind slowly turning over.

"If the school car can't get through, why not use your bike?"

"Because," said I, "I don't know how to ride one."

The administration phoned as soon as I put the phone down. "Do you know where Marc is? We have a seat for him on the same flight as the Howards tomorrow, but we need his passport to get the ticket." I told them he had gone to the Great Wall Hotel. It was too bad.

I told them about the Canadian evacuation flight tomorrow and that I would have to miss it. When could they get me out? The next flight was Sunday, 11 June. What about getting me to any west coast city, and I would fend for myself from there? There was a possibility of Friday or Saturday. They would try.

An hour later I was booked to fly to Los Angeles on

Friday (9 June). I felt that I had regained control of my life.

In the evening I went to the tuck shop for some yogurt. It was shuttered and dark as most of the campus is now. As I crossed the road to the quadrangle, Professor C— wobbled toward me on his bicycle. We almost collided in the gloom. Chinese cyclists ride without lights. He yelled something at me, then recognizing me, got off, apologized and shook my hand.

I did not like him when I first met him. He had the "lean and hungry look" of a hyena, though it was carefully camouflaged behind wreaths of smiles. He had survived the Cultural Revolution, and scratched his way to an associate professorship. He was a rabid communist who had changed sides when the hunger strike began. From then on he was active on the side of the students. He organized rallies, led sit-ins at the gates of Zhongnanhai where the leaders live. He was everywhere. Since Sunday afternoon he had been going from one hospital to another looking for students. He was near collapse but determined to continue the search. I suggested using a phone. "I don't have one," he said, "and I can't tie up the office line." "Then use mine," I suggested. He accepted readily. I poured us the last of the Glen—then took turns on the phone wheedling, and begging hospitals for information trying to find students still missing.

7 June 1989   The Howards, Dick and Maisy are gone. Veronica has been moved to a hotel by the international organization she works for. The Japanese left after a false start. As the school bus pulled out of the campus gate a convoy was coming down the highway, firing at random. They quickly turned back. The Japanese are indefatigable photographers. This respite was another chance for group photos in front of the building: with the staff; with their well-wishers; with the driver and the interpreter. Finally, the convoy passed and they piled into the bus again, waving and shouting *"Sayonara! Sayonara!"* The little lady who lived upstairs from me, smiled through her tears and waved.

I bowed. We had never exchanged more than a *"Ni hao"* a whole year, it being the entire vocabulary of a common language. There are only Judy, Diane, Edward and I left. And Edward hasn't been seen since Saturday night.

There is still the rattle of gunfire and the thud of artillery in the distance. The foos are whispering that Deng Xiaoping is dead. The army is fighting among itself in the western suburbs, and people talk ominously of civil war.

The empty school is getting on my nerves. Helicopters hover overhead constantly, sometimes so low that I can see the soldier and the glint of sunlight bouncing off the muzzle of his automatic weapon. Everyone keeps to his own apartment. Nobody speaks to anyone else.

I am packed. I will carry only the things I will need when I get home, plus my computer and printer. The rest, the institute will ship if I do not come back next semester.

A knock on the door made me leap out of my skin. It was my first assistant, W—. He had been working at one of the tourist hotels, but the guests were all gone, so he was back on campus. He had been told I was leaving, and came by to see if he could help in any way.

I needed tape and rope so we went out the north gate to the market. Only a few peddlers were out displaying a handful of half green tomatoes, and scrawny cabbages. The shops were all shuttered, but one had its iron shutters open a crack and we squeezed through. The startled shopkeeper was glad enough to take my money.

A funeral procession from our neighboring campus was moving slowly down the road. Two young men led the procession holding a huge wreath with the photograph of the dead young man mounted in its center. Across the top were four characters which meant "his spirit lives on." The mourners were all students, with strips of white cloth tied around their heads.

Suddenly there was a sputter of engines. A helicopter swooped down out of nowhere and hovered overhead. Wang gripped my arm and tugged me across the road. The procession had stopped.

"Quickly, quickly." W— dragged me through the gates,

and did not slacken his pace until we were past the playing field and into the quadrangle.

Awhile ago the phone rang. It was my son Nick, sounding so close that he might have been in the next room.

It was only after I heard myself telling him, "I'm going home on Friday," that departure has become a reality. My duffle bag is packed. The printer is in its box. Clothes, books and things have been put in closets. The apartment is almost as it was when I arrived ten months ago. But some part of me remains. The odor of pipe tobacco is here. The sound of Beethoven, Brahms, Mahler and Wagner and Strauss is here. Most of all the voices, the laughter, the footsteps, the hope and the despair of a handful of young people is here. Soaked up by the walls and the floor and furniture. Could I come back to this place? Would I have the strength—the courage to? I wish I knew.

8 June 1989   Food supply is getting low on campus. I overheard the old chef saying that we might run out of fuel as well. We had dumplings for lunch. The old man came out of the kitchen beaming. He is a kindly soul, who always has a cheery word and twinkle in his eye. There were only three diners, and the room felt cavernous. The old man came over and shook us each by the hand. "We'll do the best we can," he said. We thanked him.

I cleared all the canned food, some cereal, cheese and eggs out of my kitchen and went looking for Edward.

He came to the door red-eyed and dishevelled. His face was covered with the stubble of several days' growth. He was haggard. I explained I am leaving and thought he might like to have some extra food.

"Yes. It will come in handy." He took the two plastic bags from me into the kitchen and immediately sorted the cache into separate piles. "These I'll eat," he said, "and those . . ." He caught himself, and swallowed the rest.

We went into the living room. Edward made coffee and brought out some English biscuits. We talked about Mateo

Ricci, and about the Chinese-baroque art of Giuseppe Castiglione. These were Jesuits who had come to China in the
early Qing dynasty to preach. Both were learned men; one
a scientist, the other an artist. Emperor Qianlong recognized Castiglione's genius and made him court artist. His
job was to teach Chinese artists to paint in the European
style. However, he was also forced to work according to
Chinese custom and tradition. Ricci and Castiglione were
probably the earliest foreign experts in China. Nothing has
really changed from those days. We come here to teach, but
we too are hemmed in by outdated Chinese methods, where
everything is learnt by rote; where the teacher is never chal-
lenged; where the brain is deliberately left to rust.

Edward had been visiting his friend, a Frenchman who
has an apartment in the city, and got stranded on Saturday.
All Sunday the soldiers searched the city center for survivors. Even the building where the Frenchman lived was
searched. There was sporadic fighting in the street. Units of
the army were said to be shooting each other. Edward was
finally able to leave on Tuesday afternoon riding a bicycle
borrowed from the Frenchman. Armed stragglers roamed
the streets. For a time there was no electricity, water or
telephone service. Public transportation was paralyzed, but
a few taxis were picking up fares and charging ridiculous
prices. He was stopped several times and searched by soldiers. The streets were littered with burnt-out wrecks of
buses and cars; a few tanks and APCs too, some with
corpses in them. He saw the charred body of a soldier
dangling from a lamppost, who had been lynched and set
aflame. He had to stop and take shelter at some houses he
knew along the way, and finally got to the institute yesterday.

We talked about leaving. Edward said he would stay
until the end of his contract in July. "There won't be any
more classes," I pointed out. "And it might not be safe."
"When my friend tells me it's time to go, I will," Edward
was adamant.

"How will your friend know when it's no longer safe to
stay?"

Edward's face opened in a rare smile that was almost beatific. The sunlight behind him caught the shock of pale blonde hair and made it glow like a halo.

Suddenly the mystery of Edward was very clear. The man knew both Latin and Greek. He knew all the holy days of the Catholic calendar. He does not drink, eats very abstemiously, does not dance, has no interest in women. He has been studying the lives of Ricci and Castiglione and the work of other Jesuits in China.

Aloud, I said, "Edward, are you a priest?" He blushed and for a moment looked boyish and vulnerable. "I'll be ordained in August." "A Jesuit?" He nodded. He had not come to proselytize, he said, but to observe the work of the underground church which still has ties with the Vatican.

I had a sudden need to unburden myself. All the things I've seen and done and heard in the last seven weeks were pressing outward until my brain, indeed, my entire body ached. But it was neither the time nor the place. Perhaps if it were the dark, confining anonymity of the confessional, I might have opened up to Edward. But not across a coffee table with a can of English biscuits between us.

The moment passed. I think we both realized that the less we revealed of ourselves the better for both of us.

In the evening Professor Z— and his wife invited me for a farewell dinner. It was the first simple meal I have had in their home. Both husband and wife are workaholics, but in these days of enforced idleness Z— has been experimenting in the kitchen, and produced a splendid meal with a small piece of pork and vegetables.

The propaganda broadcasts have begun. I had already seen the telecast, but was subjected to it again with the Z—s. The announcer began saying the Square had been cleared "with the help of soldiers." Soldiers were shown sweeping the Square and scrubbing the monument. The camera zoomed in and lingered on bullet holes in the monument, and black stains on the white flagstones at its base. Panning out across the empty Square, a huge black heap could be seen smoldering in the distance. The students were called thugs now. Out of context they could be made to seem as if they were.

There were shots of students stopping a tank on the Square and setting fire to it. For a brief moment, a restlessly panning camera caught a tank rolling over students and the statue toppling over. Changan Street looked like Beirut, lined with burnt out buses, trucks and tanks. The camera lingered on the body of a soldier who had been disembowelled and hanged. The cold-eyed commander of the 27th Army came on camera and announced that five-hundred soldiers were killed by counterrevolutionaries. Only twenty-five of the general population were killed, "because the army had used extreme caution." The cameras followed Li Peng and several unnamed old dodderers as they visited wounded soldiers in an army hospital, tears running down their faces. Then there were shots of soldiers helping old ladies with bound feet across streets, and the repeated litany, "The army loves the people—the people love the army."

The Z—s watched in stony silence through most of it, screeching, "Thugs! thugs!" and shaking their fists at the screen every time a student appeared. I was horrified. Two weeks ago they were marching in support of the student movement. A week ago when we met briefly, they had talked optimistically of changes and a better future because of the movement. Now it was a complete about-face. I endured the awful film to the end, made my excuses and left.

9 June 1989   Judy got up at the crack of dawn to wave goodbye. The old chef and some of the foos stood in the doorway, looking on, smiling uncertainly. Diane, the young Mormon and I climbed on the school bus with the interpreter. As we drove out the campus gate, soldiers were getting off a lorry parked by the roadside. We gathered speed and zoomed past. The young Mormon, who had his camera poised to photograph the soldiers, was flung out of his seat. He picked himself up cursing. "How did you grow to that size without growing up?" I snapped. "Maybe it's because I've never been married," he replied with a smirk.

We threaded our way through villages, and dirt roads, avoiding the main highway. The driver muttered that his fuel was running low, and none of the gas stations nearby were open. He would have to switch off the cooling system, and use the auxiliary tank.

The airport was bedlam. Under the watchful eye of armed police, long lines sidled toward wickets, where ha-rassed airline employees pulled tickets and tagged baggage. The interpreter got us through the turnstiles and formalities of departure. I thanked her for all her help. "You will be back," she smiled. "Things will be better in the fall." I wonder. The three of us were going our separate ways. I hugged Diane and bid her farewell. The young Mormon disappeared into the crowd without saying goodbye. I joined the torrent flowing toward the boarding gates. I was returning to my other world, my other life.

I did not look back.

▶

I sat on the plane, watched a silly movie, and cried. I was physically and emotionally exhausted. The first few days, I cried a lot. One night, as I watched a replay of the Tiananmen evacuation on the evening news, a horrible keening sound filled the room. Suddenly, I realized the sound was coming from me. That realization did not stop the howling. When it finally subsided, I felt cleansed.

When I first came home, the news was full of China. But we live in violent times and people forget quickly once the shooting stops. And lies repeated often enough take on the semblance of truth. There are people I know and respect who have asked, albeit sheepishly, "Did it really happen?" That is what a campaign of lies can do to people. A German colleague who has returned to Beijing wrote: "I am no longer sure what really happened." Yes, there was a mas-sacre. Although I was not witness to the killing, I have recorded here what some survivors experienced. I will quote from a letter from my friend Pieter writing from Germany: "That Saturday night I was on my way home about ten miles west of Tiananmen when they came. I quickly drove into the nearest courtyard gate and hid the car behind two walls, and the two of us hid somewhere else. We saw them shoot at everything — and everybody was a 'thing' to them. We saw jeeps and lorries ablaze. It was a nightmare. After more than an hour of army vehicles passing by, it was over. There were two young men lying near the gate, unconscious in a pool of blood. We put them into my car. One in the boot and one on the back seat. I made a red cross with blood on a white T-shirt and drove to the nearest hospital. There were already about six dead and thirty wounded. There were many more to come."

It is frustrating that even those who condemn Deng and his henchmen miss the point of the movement. The democracy the students clamored for is not the Western (or American) system of government. That has been tried before and failed. Democracy cannot succeed in a fuedal society. Nor can it succeed in a society where a large segment of the population is illiterate and incapable of forming political opinions. At no time did the students advocate overthrowing the regime. They merely demanded that it set its house in order so that the vaunted ideas of reform and progress can take place. They demanded the right to pursue life to its fullest potential. These I see as positive demands. For only when youth are permitted to chose education and careers suited to their talents can abundant human resources benefit society.

Many of us in the West see this tragedy as a blow against communism. Perhaps it will become the thin end of the wedge. Only history can tell. To change a form of government there must be an alternative. Right now China has no alternative.

The institute and a handful of young people, whose names I must keep secret for their sakes and mine, is a microcosm of the movement. That is why their story had to be told.

The righteous indignation of the West when the atrocities occurred was to cut off economic support. Indeed it was the only means available to the West of registering its shock and disapproval. Richard Nixon's was the first voice raised against such a ploy. He was right. China and its aging leaders have been isolated from the world so long that condemnation from the whole world would not touch them, even when it hurts them in the pocketbook where they are most sensitive. Such a plan will only drive China to shrink into herself and in the process the people will suffer.

In the months between, a tight lid has been clamped on China. None of the young people mentioned in this book have been heard from except X—, who is well and back at his university. A— never resurfaced after 3 June, or if he did I have not heard. J— and the others who went underground are silent. I only hope that no news is good news.

Going underground is no easy feat. Once more, people are informing on one another, often settling petty personal grudges with official sanction. This is a form of terrorism that began in the Tang dynasty (A.D. 618–907) and is still effective centuries later, which reinforces the idea that China has not changed. Still, bits of news leak out. Another foreign colleague who remained after the rest of us had left wrote from Beijing:

"I had certain tenuous links with students and staff from the university, mostly by phone. I was particularly concerned with ensuring that everyone was safe and stayed that way. So far, it appears that one student died in the massacre and at least two were arrested when they returned home and were overheard 'spreading rumors.' However, I'm sure that's not the end of it. The university started up again with a week of political study and writing confessions. Except in the most flagrant cases—membership in illegal student unions, leadership in student action, speaking to foreign journalists—I think the government intends to menace but not to terrorize. Teaching starts tomorrow to make up for last term's work. Several phone calls confirm the predictable consequences of the last few months' events: fear and depression. I'm dreading even trying to carry on teaching English as if it was a valid subject of study under the present circumstances."

Political studies, a euphemism for propaganda, have been brought back to the classrooms. Graduating students are sent to rural areas for at least one year of manual labor before they go to their assigned jobs. Freshmen require one full year of military training. All this harks back to the dark days of the Cultural Revolution. China has taken a giant step backwards.

At the end of July, Chinese radio and television reported the breakup of one of the country's largest trading companies, the Kanhua Development Corporation, headed by Deng's wheelchair-bound son Deng Pufang. A shakeup of other companies was promised. In another move to bolster Party spirit and the people's aspirations, the Politburo ordered an end to banquets, bribes, foreign travel, and the use of luxury cars by officials. Limits were also set on what their children could do for a living. Henceforth, official trips abroad must be for work only, and not "inspection,"a euphemism for tourism.

Arrests, trials and executions continue. Wu'er Kaixi, one of the leaders of the movement escaped to France. Chai Ling, the fiery young woman leader, has been reported variously as living in hiding somewhere in China, or in Australia. Wang Dan was arrested. Hou Dejian, the rock singer, who created a stir when he defected from Taiwan in 1985, and who negotiated with the commandant to allow the students to withdraw from the Square shortly before the massacre began, came out of hiding two months later. Looking relaxed and happy on national television, he glibly denied seeing any bloodshed on the Square.

Once more, rumors are rife that Deng is dead or near death. There is perhaps some truth in this in the light of the sudden detention of a number of army chiefs who were in Beijing for a high-level conference and preparations for Zhao Zhiyang's show trial.

In the meantime, the Square has been scoured. A thin trickle of tourists has reappeared. Disaster is a great magnet for tourism. Soon the cash registers will ring louder than ever, and the blood and sinew of the faceless masses will be swept away and forgotten.

Except by a few. A very, very few.

Vancouver, British Columbia
27 August 1989

Epilogue

It had rained all day. Though it had stopped by the time the plane landed, the ground was still wet and patches of mist slithered close to the ground. Everything smelled dank. The two people from the institute who met me were genuinely glad to see me. There are fewer "experts" now, and fewer foreign students too.

When I left three months ago, I did not think I would ever see my campus apartment again. Yet here I am and everything is where I left it. There was even half a pot of tea with green things floating on it. In the fridge, I found half a baguette, a square of rancid butter, and a few spoonfuls of instant coffee in a jar. The foo had scoured the apartment and the smell of detergents was heavy in the air. After my greeters left, silence closed in, thick and stifling. It was unnerving. I put on the first tape that I laid hands on. Anything to fill the void. The music swirled round the apartment, darting in and out of the shadows, scurling round the walls, rousing all the ghosts. It took a long time to relax enough to go to bed.

I woke before dawn not knowing where I was. I must have been sleeping with my mouth open, for my throat was dry and my palate felt like parchment. I stumbled into the kitchen for water. Now I was wide awake. I lay there watching the sky lighten and the sparrows gather on my window sill, wondering what the day would bring.

After weeks of starts and stops, my teaching schedule finally settled to a dull roar. I am continuing the task of developing a text. However, I am not teaching the seniors as I expected. They have weightier fish to fry before they graduate. Instead, I have the entire junior year; seventy passive, and blank-faced young people who soak up everything like sponges without question. The ghetto-blasters are silent. Students come and go singly or in pairs. Nobody talks. There is an occasional burst of song sounding raucous and angry, stopping as suddenly as it started. The campus is bleak.

The timetables are jam-packed with new courses on ideology and philosophy. One Friday afternoon I arrived and found the classroom locked. At five after two when no one appeared I went searching for the dean. The man is looking terribly harassed these days. To my question, "Where is my class?" all he could supply was a blank stare. We scurried down the corridor, opening and shutting doors. Finally, at the head of the stairs we found a hastily scrawled note on the bulletin board. The entire junior year was required to attend a new philosophy course Friday afternoons. The dean looked apologetic. I was angry. We went back to the office and pored over the junior year's schedule. Every slot was taken. Would I teach in the evening? No, said I. Students would be too tired to take in anything. Would I teach on Saturday? No, again. My contract specifies that I do not teach Saturday or Sunday. In the end, the philosophy course was re-scheduled.

There is a tacit silence about the seniors I taught.

"They've all graduated," said the dean, "and have jobs." He smiled and it was clear the subject was closed. It is as though J— , and A— and all the others never existed.

Now and then I come across students I taught before. They wave and smile. I wave and smile, and a chasm yawns between. I make no attempt to bridge it. One must try to be objective. They know where they may venture and I do not.

There is no trust between these young people. The drivel overheard in corridors that passes for conversation, is pathetic. The loneliness is palpable. H—, whom I taught as a junior, was one of the few who first came to visit me. Last summer burnt off what he had left of baby fat. He is lean and pasty, already worn down by the semester, which started in mid-July and will last till mid-January without a break.

H— was not a serious student. Personal charm and background would get him where he wanted to be. But now he is not so sure. Next summer he will graduate, and like many others, will learn the virtues of labor in the countryside for a year or two before he enters his chosen profession.

"By then I would have forgotten everything I ever learnt," he lamented.

H— used to be popular. Now he has no friends. "There is no one to talk to and nothing worth saying," he sighs. Everyone watches and listens.

The reading rooms of the library are always full. There is nowhere else to go; not even a coffee shop. Now that the new austerity has banned the Saturday night dances, and winter has set in, life is becoming a grey monotony. Sometimes I stop to watch the boys play soccer on my way home from class. They play with such fury, kicking and elbowing, that one wonders what is going through their minds. Tempers are short. One day, someone tried to jump the queue at the canteen at lunchtime, and a brawl ensued in which personal scores were settled.

There was an invitation from the National Foreign Experts Bureau on my desk when I arrived. The occasion was a reception at the Great Hall of the People to celebrate the fortieth anniversary of the founding of the People's Republic. The European experts refused to attend; a stupid and quixotic gesture that does not win friends or influence people. However, the rest of us got out our best bib and tucker, and were driven in the late afternoon to the Great Hall, past the deserted Square, the shiny helmets and the white gloves, and the gleaming muzzles pointed skyward. I had been to the Great Hall two years ago on a cold, blustery day. It was dark and full of echoes, overpowering in its massiveness. But with the chandeliers ablaze and a deep red carpet sweeping up the white marble stairs, it no longer oppressed.

White-linen-covered tables filled the banquet hall. We took our seats according to location numbers. At the far end of the room, a green-uniformed orchestra held forth with patriotic selections. The playing was better than the material. Men in turbans and women in saris mingled with brightly-colored caftans and richly embroidered kimonos. A dozen languages were spoken at once. The orchestra struck up a martial tune, the black velvet curtain that hid a door at the far end slowly parted, and the official party led by Mr. Li entered the hall. Someone announced the beginning of the reception, and everybody rose for the national anthem.

The short speech by the vice premier, Liu, expressed the country's appreciation of the efforts of its foreign friends. There was a toast, and we set about the serious business of eating. The food was excellent. The orchestra regaled us with more oom-pa-pa with Chinese characteristics. "On the Beautiful Blue Danube" brought a warm round of applause. This was followed by the "Radetsky March." However, just as the Lepizan horses were about to hit their stride, the official party rose to leave. The orchestra scrambled into suitable oom-pa-pa; the black velvet curtains rose and fell and they were gone. Chinese banquets always end abruptly. We drove home through almost empty streets. It was barely eight o'clock.

A few weeks later, the institute celebrated its anniversary. There was a big celebration: sports events, concerts and exhibitions to which foreigners were cordially not invited. However, we did get trotted out to a gala closing event. Heads of ministries and former presidents so ancient they did not know where they were gathered in the auditorium. The president gave a forty-five-minute address in which he enumerated the institute's achievements. Only the last few lines of the speech were worth hearing. Said he: "We have learned a valuable lesson. Many errors came from outside. We must be on guard to stamp them out. Only then can we consider improving the quality of education . . . "

In November the military was withdrawn. Armed police and security guards in smart blue uniforms patrol the streets. The Square is still closed. But the city is less grim. Wang-fujing is crowded but one is not pushed along. Prices have dropped, but few are buying. *China Daily* says there is more pork available than we can possibly eat. However, in the same article it says farmers are not raising pigs because the price of meat cannot keep up with the price of feed. There is a lot of coal, but every Friday there is neither heat, light or water on campus. The invasion of the cabbages has begun. *China Daily* says 300 million tons were shipped to the city. However, cabbage is out of fashion this year and only 220 million tons have been sold. The surplus has been palmed off on work units which in turn palm it off on employees. They're even selling cabbage at gas stations.

The city is bereft of tourists. There were only six people in the Beijing Hotel lounge on a Sunday afternoon. Three Arabs giggling in a corner. A Brit reading a week-old *Guardian* and sipping tea. A very drunk American woman of indeterminate vintage trying to grope the waiter. And me.

The one glimmer of hope is the Asian Games. But the facilities are nowhere near completion and there is no money. Everybody is "buying" bonds to raise funds. Students and others have been donating their time to help with the building. A group of senior citizens were seen on the evening news aimlessly shovelling earth. One old fellow in his eighties who was singled out for attention, blinked and mumbled at the camera dazed and exhausted. He seemed to be going round in circles. Aren't we all?

One bitterly cold afternoon in November A— appeared. He was very thin, and looked far from well. It was time to break out the Scotch.

"I'm glad you're back," he said. The lopsided grin was still there, but the cockiness was missing. The eyes were black and opaque. The long fingered hands fidgeted. He chain-smoked, and talked in short bursts, his voice pitched so low I had to strain to hear him. After the long exhausting summer, he was finally assigned a job and allowed to graduate. But there is no work, so there is no pay. He was singing in a cafe until someone stole his guitar. Now he was keeping himself alive with odd jobs. It was only when he spoke of his music that the old spark flared in his eyes. The dream lives.

J— wrote from the south: "I have a job taking care of the

public toilets and the flowers in a hotel. Later I might move into housekeeping, or dishwashing and maybe be a bellboy if I'm lucky." He worries about his brain atrophying, so he is teaching himself Western art. From him I hear that Y— has gone home to his village to be a school teacher. M— has broken with her family and is soon to be married. Willie, who dreamed of becoming a minor bureaucrat, is teaching "Ing-a-leesh" as he calls it, to waiters of a restaurant. The others are scattered across the country.

One afternoon, as I crossed the quadrangle to my apartment, I saw G— reading on one of the benches. He did not look up until I sat down beside him. "I heard you were back, and I wondered when we'd meet." "I'm in the same apartment." The mouth in the mask-like face quivered. "I don't know what to say." "There's no need to say anything." He fumbled with a pack of cigarettes, lit two and handed me one. We smoked in silence. "You're all right, and I'm all right," he said after a long silence. "It's important to stay alive." I got up. We clasped hands. "Take care," I said. He nodded. A handful of dry leaves, caught by a gust of wind, danced across the quadrangle ahead of me.

About the Author:

Michael David Kwan was born in Beijing in 1934. Trained as a social worker, Mr. Kwan worked with refugee populations in Hong Kong in the 1950s. Since then he has worked as a writer and producer of classical music programs for Radio Hong Hong and as a senior consultant for a travel service in Vancouver, where he makes his home. His interest in writing stems from the extensive Chinese-English translations he has completed over the years, including OLD WELL, by Zheng Yi and BEST CHINESE STORIES 1949–1989 from Chinese Literature Press. Currently he is teaching and developing a tourism course in Beijing as well as working on various translating and writing projects.

GOOD DEEDS & GUNBOATS
Two Centuries of American-Chinese Encounters
by Hugh Deane

A collection of Chinese encounters by famous American missionaries, businessmen, opium merchants, poets, singers, soldiers and journalists, reveals the formation of American perceptions toward China over the last 200 years.

#2378-2   cloth $24.95

CHINA BORN
Adventures of a Maverick Bookman
by Henry Noyes

The autobiography of the founder of China Books & Periodicals, Inc. chronicles Noyes' life and his dealings with China as he struggled against the fanaticism of the McCarthy era to found what was to become the largest importer, distributor and publisher of books from and about mainland China.

#2045-7   cloth $16.95
#2034-1   paper $ 9.95

TEACHING CHINA'S LOST GENERATION
by Tani E. Barlow and Donald M. Lowe

Unique experiences and insights of two professors teaching American literature and society in China during the '80s, whose students were largely victims of China's Cultural Revolution.

#1818-5   paper $9.95

CHINESE PROFILES
by Zhang Xinxin and Sang Ye
Forty candid interviews of "ordinary" Chinese men and women.
#1603-4   paper $8.95

TWO YEARS IN THE MELTING POT
by Liu Zongren
A Chinese journalist's account of living in America for two years, whose initial culture shock and attempt to come to terms with life in the U.S. offer a unique way for Americans to look at themselves.

#2048-1   cloth $16.95
#2035-X   paper $ 9.95

MORNING BREEZE
A True Story of China's Cultural Revolution
by Fulang Lo
The compelling autobiography of a young woman caught up in the chaos of the Cultural Revolution and her eventual disillusionment with Mao.

#2125-9   cloth $16.95
#2126-7   paper $ 9.95

6 TANYIN ALLEY
by Liu Zongren
A fictional account of the lives of Beijing families sharing a courtyard, caught up in the momentum of the Cultural Revolution.

#2146-1   cloth $17.95

PRISONERS OF LIBERATION
by Allyn and Adele Rickett

A personal account of two Americans convicted of espionage in China in 1949 and their transformation through reform.

#0819-8   paper $9.95

OLD WELL
by Zheng Yi

The controversial novel about two desperately poor lovers, clinging to the parched land of their ancestors, who draw on inner courage in a tragic attempt to remain together in a village entrenched in poverty, bloody sacrifice and legend.

#2275-1   cloth $16.95
#2276-X   paper $ 8.95

LAPSE OF TIME
by Wang Anyi

A volume of short stories dealing with the problems of young people whose lives were disrupted by the Cultural Revolution, and who now face the practical realities of modern China.

#2031-7   cloth $16.95
#2932-5   paper $ 8.95

LOVE MUST NOT BE FORGOTTEN
by Zhang Jie

A selection of short stories from China's foremost woman
writer. Considered to be China's first feminist writer, she
treats controversial themes with insight and unusual sensitiv-
ity.

> #1699-9 cloth $16.95
> #1698-0 paper $ 8.95

THE PIANO TUNER
by Cheng Naishan

Touching stories of love, family and the urban business class
of Shanghai from the first openly proclaimed Christian to
achieve national literary status in China.

> #2142-9 cloth $16.95
> #2141-0 paper $ 8.95

QUOTATIONS FROM CHAIRMAN MAO TSETUNG

This facsimile edition of Mao's "Little Red Book" in English
makes interesting reading, especially in light of the recent
events of China. Mao may be gone, but definitely not forgotten.

> #2377-4 original red plastic cover $7.95

•

Write or call today for our free mail-order catalog which
includes a whole array of gifts and books from and about
China.

2929 Twenty-fourth Street • San Francisco, CA 94110
(415) 282-2994 • FAX (415) 282-0994